INNER SKY

LIFE BEGINS WHERE

RESISTANCE ENDS

I dedicate this book to …

My mother Catherine Layer, born into an incredibly challenging life situation which became her ongoing suffering and my biggest teaching about resistance. I thank you for your endless love and dedication to my brothers and I beyond everything you faced. How your life played out was no accident. Its lessons and hidden wisdoms come alive in this book, and will guide all those who read it. You are not only my mother, you are a teacher for the many.

To Dr. Rahasya Fritjof Kraft, master, teacher and friend. Behind all of your teachings is the subtle message of resistance, that which keeps us from living. Thank you for guiding me through the dark valleys of my life, where 'the little me' was physically and metaphysically dying and transformed into living. This book is a dedication to you and your teachings, which enabled me to invite the unknown to my table and experience the spontaneous cure of cancer. Thank you my friend for bringing me back to life and living, and for your guidance that allowed me to realise the love that I am.

First published in 2017 by Layer Consulting Pty Ltd.

National Library of Australia Cataloguing-in-Publication data has been applied for.

    978-0-6480266-0-0 (Print)
    978-0-6480266-1-7 (Ingram)
    978-0-6480266-4-8 (Createspace)
    978-0-6480266-2-4 (ePub)
    978-0-6480266-3-1 (mobi)

Cover image © iStock
Front cover and internal design by Natalie Winter.
www.captainhoney.com.au

Printed and bound in Australia by Griffin Press

5 4 3 2 1   17 18 19 20 21

STEVEN LAYER (Premdas)

INNER SKY

LIFE BEGINS WHERE

RESISTANCE ENDS

A conversation about resistance.

With the teachings of Dr. Rahasya Fritjof Kraft
as experienced by Steven Layer.

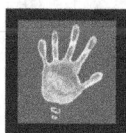

Contents

Prelude

Who am I to share what I saw looking directly into the face of mortality? Yet in becoming still and seeing, what was incurable was cured in an instant. Who Am I? The question that points us inwards for the answers.

If I had one afternoon to spend with a friend who was facing a life-threatening illness, what would I say?

This is that conversation.

~ 1 ~

Incurable means inward curable

I am just a normal guy who enjoys watching the footy, surfing and having a few beers with his mates on the weekend. I never asked for this to happen to me, but it happened just the same. Life has a way of taking you on a journey designed just for you. Destiny is what people call it, a beautiful and often challenging journey where you are the main character in your own story.

I thought I would follow my father's footsteps and live a conservative life of an engineer. Society in middle-class America programmed me with certain goals: to be successful in a material way, have a good dependable job, find a wife and have children, buy a house in the suburbs and raise my kids and of course be a responsible provider. The end goal was to eventually grow old and retire to a life with money in the bank and not too much to do except rake the leaves on a cold autumn day and play a few rounds of golf with my buddies.

So off I went following this path without really questioning anything, with a lack of awareness about what I really wanted out of life. After growing up in the leafy suburbs of Boston USA, I went to university and received a practical diploma in Accounting and Information Systems. I worked for a number of years as a Systems Engineer and met a woman who I loved very much. By the age of 28, I was well on my way to fulfilling 'the dream' from an external point of view.

I met Angelina in Sydney Australia, soon after arriving from Boston to work on a software development project. A little over a year later we married and settled in the northern beaches of the city. In the first year of our marriage, I took a bold step and set up my own software consultancy company. After about nine years of running that business, everything I dreamed of seemed to be coming true. I had a beautiful wife and two adorable children, a house a few blocks from the beach, and a growing business. I had also just landed a big software development contract with the largest recruitment company in Australia.

By the age of 38 my life seemed perfect. This is why when I was confronted with advanced cancer I reacted to it in a way many people would: first with shock, then disbelief. After the shock waves passed, I wanted to run away from it as fast as I could while at the same time kill it. This thing called cancer instantly became my enemy and was going to destroy everything I had worked for, at the very moment in my life where happiness was finally within my grasp. To hold onto what I had, I knew I had to fight cancer.

Running away and fighting was quite normal for me. Fight or flight is what they call it, avoid or defeat the things in life that confront us. I was particularly adept at avoiding what I didn't want in my life, but I soon discovered that I couldn't avoid cancer because it had become a part of me. So I turned to fight it. As I faced this new enemy, something peculiar happened. The need to treat cancer as the enemy and defeat it suddenly shifted, a kind of miracle happened ... and my cancer spontaneously cured.

This experience changed the way I perceived things. Soon afterwards I started questioning a lot of things about the life I was living and everything society had told me to be. As a result, I made a lot of changes, including the decision to step away from my business.

I asked myself, "What am I doing?" and "What do I really want to do?" In the years following cancer, I knew my heart was no longer in running my software company. I sold it to the other directors and stepped away.

My whole life I had been extremely driven to be 'successful'. I remember friends, family and the neighbours all asking me the same questions: "What are you going to do now Steven?" "Aren't you worried about the future?" "Isn't life boring without your work?" The truth was I had been so blindly driven from an early age to become 'someone', and to be 'successful', that I never allowed myself to stop 'becoming', 'achieving' and 'doing.' I had never allowed myself to pause once in the fast paced life I had created. When I sold my software business, I did it consciously for one main reason: I wanted to experience being, to see what that was like for a little while. Deep in my heart, I wanted to work with people, to share what I had learned, and to help them just as I had helped myself.

Two years went by fast and I had never been in such a beautiful and happy state, enjoying life and living outside the old habit of becoming something. I didn't drop out of society; I was still very active with my family and the community and keeping fit through surfing. Continuing to provide for my family, I made some timely investments in the stock market and took on part-time work creating websites and performing I.T. services for a handful of small companies in my local community. I was engaged yet not trying to achieve anything for any personal sense of status.

Two years soon became six and an old friend came to visit me one day. He started talking about his passion for kite surfing and asked me what my passion was now that I no longer owned my software company? The words, "Helping people free themselves" seamlessly flowed from my lips. He looked at me curiously, opened his mouth but no words came out as he was not sure what to make of my answer. Freedom can mean many things - I was talking about the freedom from the invisible cages we erect around ourselves.

It is easy to talk about the past, and the titles I held on to so tightly: Software Engineer, Business Analyst, The CEO of my own software company, Husband, Father, Son, Brother, Surfer, Baseball Coach. It is harder to put into words what I do in the present, because there is no official title, nor the need to have one.

I'm just a normal 55 year-old guy in most respects. Yet through some challenging life experiences I have found a certain freedom and enjoy helping others who are stuck or are seeking what I have found. Often all it takes is a small shift in perspective to break free from what holds us captive, be it physical, mental or spiritual.

Yesterday my dear friend Lily called me in a state of sheer panic. Hearing the distress in her voice, I jumped on a plane and flew down to Sydney to spend the afternoon with her.

Lily and I had been business colleagues, collaborating on many software projects throughout the years. I had not seen her since I sold my company, although we kept in contact by email now that I lived eight hours north of Sydney in a small country coastal town. She was in the place I had been, diagnosed with advanced cancer and facing mortality for the first time.

Lily was desperate to find out how to 'kill the cancer'. I knew how she was feeling. Back then I too wanted to fight what I was afraid of, and didn't know that cancer usually comes at the end of the line, after we have ignored the signs of our inner disharmony for far too long. Society teaches us to 'get rid of' the thing we don't want, so it is easy to want to wage a war against cancer and kill it. Yet I found another way. We don't need to fight. Nobody ever wins in war. Our darkest time is a time for understanding. In coming to understand what we perceive to be the enemy, we find a resolution and the conflict can resolve peacefully.

So I came to be with my friend Lily. I didn't come to talk to her about cancer, but to help her understand what is behind it, and what keeps us at arms length from a peaceful resolution. What I discovered through my own experience is that the solution to life's biggest challenges lies behind what appears on the surface as a symptom. Cancer, like any other challenging illness, is a symptom that reflects something else we can no longer ignore.

I had one afternoon with Lily in which I was hoping to bring a new perspective to her situation. Arriving at her house at midday she welcomed me with a wry smile. It was great to see her again even in these circumstances and I could see she was still the strong-minded businesswoman I had known previously. However there was a new softness about her, a vulnerability that I remembered from my own experience. Handing me a cup of tea, we sat at her kitchen table across from each other and took a moment to just look into each other's eyes. As the teardrops rolled down her cheeks, she moved quickly to wipe them away.

~ 2 ~

Don't shoot the messenger

Reaching for her hand I asked: "Lily, how are you? Are you coping with everything?"

The words came tumbling out …

"Steven, I am scared and everything is happening so fast. I feel like I'm in a dream. One minute life is fine, the next minute I'm dying. My doctor is pressuring me. I have to make some decisions because he wants to operate on Monday morning. Friends and family are giving me conflicting advice. I am so confused. This is why I called you, because I know you have been through this. I remember you were successful against the odds. When the doctor gave me the diagnosis last week, for some reason you came into my mind. I have so many questions and don't know where to start."

Her words jogged my memory as I felt her fear. I recalled the feeling standing on this same precipice years ago. "I'm so glad you called me. I'm here for you and will support you the best I can."

How are Peter and the girls?

The girls are a mess. Melissa is just about to take her University entrance exams. She is so stressed out with the weight of my cancer and the intensity of her final year in high school. Samantha on the other hand has become strangely quiet and just stays in her room all day long. This couldn't have come at a worse time, my girls need me more now than ever before!

And Peter?

Peter is a huge support. He is taking time off work to help, spending most of his time searching for a solution and looking after the girls. Every day he comes to me with new ideas on what to do. I know he means well, but I am so fucking confused.

I understand the confusion, I remember how everyone around me was telling me what to do. They care about you, but they are also confronted by what is happening right now. I know you want to take care of your daughters, but I suggest the best thing you can do for them right now is to focus on yourself. Let Peter look after the girls. Everyone will benefit from you helping yourself right now.

You said you were waiting on a call from your doctor, what is the situation?

This morning he said that the cancer was stage 3, and ... *[crying]* ... I have a 30% chance ...

He is not Nostradamus and he doesn't know you like I know you. So don't believe his prediction, we will investigate this together.

I remember the intensity of the situation and the pressure to make major life decisions quickly, but not knowing where to start. "You may be wondering how to even begin to deal with what's happening when cancer is staring you in the face."

Exactly! Lily says.

Do you remember when your girls were younger – did they sometimes get so worked up emotionally and have a tantrum, crying and throwing themselves on the floor, refusing just about anything you did to try and help them?

Yes.

How did you snap them out of the emotional chaos and help them to become calm again?

Well, we have a special place in the house, we call the sunny space. Over there on the bench seat built into the window. I would sit them there for 5 to 10 minutes and usually they became calm and would often fall asleep.

'Sunny space' is a great name for it. And space is exactly what you need right now. Everything is coming at you in a situation that is seemingly out of control. So I suggest you do the same thing, and find your sunny space. Take some time-out from the craziness of what is happening, find a quiet space somewhere where nobody will interrupt you, turn off your phone and become still for 10 to

30 minutes or whatever feels right and see what happens.

Finding space for yourself is a good place to start. It can help you see this situation from a new perspective. I'm here to share a new perspective on this situation called cancer. And hopefully with a new perspective, clarity of direction will replace the confusion that is here right now.

OK, she said as she wiped away more tears.

Unlike other life experiences, cancer is one that you cannot ignore or postpone. This experience asks us to stop everything else and be here right now.

Why do you call cancer an experience?

My focus is not on cancer, my focus is on Life – your life! Life is a succession of experiences and cancer is an experience that is happening in your life right now. So I like to talk about cancer as an experience, as a situation. This subtle shift can help us see things in a new way.

Most people in your situation put all of their energy into the cancer, and look at it as the enemy, something to kill and get rid of. Most people get lost in a fight and miss the whole point. Cancer is a symptom that has appeared, and it doesn't appear overnight like catching a cold after riding the city bus. It takes a period of time while other symptoms have been knocking at our door, before cancer finally appears.

Other symptoms?

More subtle symptoms, like an ongoing inner feeling of disharmony.

Let me say this another way: Lily, whatever is going on inside of us is reflected in what happens on the outside, in our physical life. You are a reflection of your emotional self.

What do you mean inside?

You know, the inner you, your inner world. The world of your thoughts, stories, emotions, desires, beliefs, fears...the world of your mind.

The outer you, is the physical you, your experiences, the dramas in your life or lack of them, your health or ill-health, your abundance or lack of it, your loving relationships or heartache. Whatever you are experiencing on the outside, is simply a reflection of the inner you.

I don't get what you are saying?

OK, let me say it a different way. If disease appears in the physical, this is a reflection of where you are already hurt on the inside. The source of that hurt is typically invisible wounds from your past experiences that you are knowingly and unknowingly holding onto.

Are you talking about physical injuries?

No, I'm talking about emotional injuries associated with painful experiences, emotional experiences that we didn't want to feel when they were happening. Over time these emotional hurts can lead to physical illnesses.

Come on, really?

Yes, I've learned that the body is created by the mind. The state of the mind and its focus creates the body. This is important to know, so we just don't look at the body as something that gets diseased out-of-the-blue. It takes time for this to occur, and the source of it starts inside, at the level of mind.

To help understand this, let me use myself as an example. I was 38 years old and on the surface life was perfect. What people saw on the outside was far from the truth of what was going on inside. To look at me you would have seen that I had everything. I even convinced myself of this because I chose to ignore what I was really feeling inside. The truth was totally different. My relationship with my wife was strained. The connection we had, that special spark in our relationship had faded. Inside I had this feeling of heaviness that had been with me since my childhood. So when trouble started brewing in my marriage I did exactly what I'd always done since childhood, and buried what I didn't want to see or feel and then threw myself into activities to divert my attention from those inner feelings. My biggest diversion was work, and I became a workaholic, telling myself that if I achieved material success, then my marriage would be full of love again and all of the pain I was feeling inside would go away.

What I falsely believed and what society is constantly reinforcing, is that happiness is just around the corner. What I found is very different. If we seek happiness only through our outer physical world, happiness always stays one step in front of us, like a carrot on a stick in front of the horse, we move forward but never quite reach it. Does this ring any bells?

Yes, but why is this?

Society teaches us to avoid pain and seek pleasure. We learn to be the judge and jury of what's happening in our life. We naturally allow pleasurable experiences, and we deny and resist those experiences we associate with pain.

This is life as we have come to know it, and society likes to divide things into 'good' or 'bad', 'should' and 'should not'. We learned 'good' and 'bad' at a very young age. When we did something our parents liked, we were 'good' and we received praise or rewards and we felt loved. When we did something our parents didn't like, we were 'bad' and were scolded or punished and felt the source of love from our parents pull away. So very early on in life we were taught to embrace things that are 'good' and avoid things that are 'bad', and we still quietly apply this to most things in our life including our outer experiences, but particularly to our inner experiences.

We judge our inner experiences?

By observing our parents and those around us, we learned that certain emotions and feelings are 'bad' and are to be avoided. When we were young if we legitimately got angry and started yelling for example, we would get punished. To avoid punishment, we learned to bury and not express certain emotions and feelings. We also learned that if we were happy and expressed that happiness we would be accepted, loved and rewarded in some way. We have absorbed these rules and learnt to freely express some emotional feelings, yet suppress and imprison others.

In short, society promotes 'the good' and demotes 'the bad', and anything deemed 'bad' is avoided, shut down, cast away or what

I call 'resisted'. We don't even think about this in our daily life anymore, as this response to life experiences has become habitual. Our automatic response to anything bad is to resist it.

We all have hurts, we all have stories and conflicts from our past that shake us up and shape our lives as we move forward. These hurts and their effect on us are nothing to be ashamed of. We are all in the same human boat, none of us are immune to being hurt, yet most of us follow what we have been taught, and find various ways to avoid our hurts.

I remember the day my life changed. It was the day I decided I would never again feel the intense hurts I was feeling inside. I was ten years old, in the fifth grade in primary school. I had a very special teacher that year, someone I knew I could go to with any problem. I desperately needed help with what was going on at home, something I didn't understand that had been quietly eating away at me through most of my childhood. One morning after a particularly emotionally painful weekend at home, I got up the courage to ask for help and wrote a note for my teacher. The note had five words written on it, and I put the note in my shirt pocket. I rode my bike to school and sat in class all day looking for just the right moment to approach my teacher. A couple of times I stood up and walked towards her, but each time I stopped myself and sat back down in my chair. When the end of school bell rang, I just couldn't do it; I couldn't deliver the note.

The note was about my mother who I loved very much, and I didn't want to betray her or get her in trouble in any way. In many ways I loved her more than I loved myself, so instead of handing in the note, I decided right then and there to grow an extra thick layer of skin and bury everything inside. I swore to myself that I would never ever feel those hurtful feelings again. From that day forward, I shut myself down to whatever was going on at home and buried any experience that brought similar feelings of pain.

Do you mind me asking, what did the note say?

It read: My Mother is an Alcoholic.

~ 3 ~

Whatever you resist persists

Are you saying those things you buried under your skin
created cancer?

Let me put it this way, ***whatever we resist persists.***[R] Hurts, tension,
or past experiences that we suppress or try to escape from don't go
away when we avoid them, they persist. In fact they get stronger and
more pronounced the longer we resist them.

We might be able to avoid the feelings for a period of time, but
it's only a postponement. Eventually life will bring us a situation
that we can no longer postpone. Cancer is one of those life
situations we can't avoid, bringing with it the message: 'Enough
is enough, stop running from yourself.' I know this might sound
strange at this moment, but the situation you find yourself in can be
an opportunity, a blessing in disguise, to welcome home what you
haven't met inside. This is what I found.

[R] Dr. Rahasya Fritjof Kraft

18

Come on! ... why would I want to welcome pain?

As we meet whatever we are resisting, it dissolves. I realise this is hard to believe, but it is true. My story is probably the best way to bring this to light.

What do you mean 'whatever we are resisting'?

What I am talking about here is how we avoid or allow experiences in life and their related feelings, emotions and sensations. Like when I was in the fifth grade in a very difficult family situation, I didn't know how to deal with what was happening. I didn't know how to handle the shock and other emotions I was feeling, so instead of getting help, I resisted. I buried the feelings, thoughts and memories inside me, never to be felt again.

This is resistance?

Yes. Let me give you another example to help you understand resistance. Take yourself back to when you were 25 years old. Say you were deeply in love with your boyfriend who you consider to be your soul mate. You go to a beach one day, and he gets down on one knee, pulls out a wedding ring and asks you to marry him. You lovingly accept his proposal. Later that day, you get back to your apartment and you share the exciting news with all your friends and family. This is an example of a life experience that you allow. You embrace the experience, feel your feelings, and it flows through you without any resistance.

Now, let's look at another experience. Say you have been married for ten years and you discover that your husband has been cheating on you with your best friend. You confront your husband and he confirms that it is true, and in the same breath he tells you he doesn't love you, wants a divorce and is going to marry your friend. In this confronting situation, you will likely have a wave of emotions and feel a lot of pain, betrayal, abandonment, and anger and the situation can easily put you into shock. Our automatic conditioned tendency is to want to 'get rid of' the pain or to suppress it. *Any way we are not with our experience in the moment it arises is resistance.*

> So what? This cancer can kill me and I don't want it! I want to escape and wake up to find it was all a bad dream. This is resistance?

Wanting to escape from something that is here right now is a common resistance.

Resistance is found in all the ways we try to avoid, escape, suppress or fight the thoughts, sensations and emotional feelings related to our experiences. We resist in all sorts of ways. We blame other people for what's happening, we tell stories and gossip about them, and we may even fight the other person. We might use self pity, taking on the role of a victim to escape our experience, or we might ignore the experience itself and say it doesn't bother us. We may stay super busy as a diversion from feeling what is happening inside. Work, TV and excessive sleep are common ways we avoid. Addictions are also a common resistance. People turn to Alcohol, Drugs, Food, Sex, Work as a means to escape their inner pain. We might become controlling, and try to manage everything and everyone around us to ensure we don't relive hurts associated with our past that get triggered by experiences in the present. In my case, I suppressed my experiences so deeply under my skin that the experience became repressed. What I mean by that is the painful experience was denied to such a degree, that over time I not only forgot what was buried, I convinced myself that the discord inside was normal and no problem existed. However, like a beacon emitting an invisible warning signal, those things we resist regularly let us know that something is there that needs attention. We feel it as an inner disharmony, knowing it is there but often not knowing what it is.

> But isn't this just life, I mean I am a very busy woman...what's the harm in escaping painful experiences and getting on with things?

The harm is in the ongoing disharmony we experience. You are sitting in front of me right now with cancer. This is a perfect example. Physical disease is a type of disharmony. And disharmony not only comes at the physical level, it also comes at the mental and spiritual level. In fact, it shows up in the area of your mind first and progresses to the physical through our resistance. Without resistance, we would simply experience whatever is happening, and our experiences would come and go like the passing of a cloud in the sky.

> So you are saying that my cancer is a result of me avoiding something else, and that it starts out in the mind and ends up as cancer? You have got to be joking!

My observation is that a large portion of physical health issues are derived out of what first appears in our point of view, our psyche: emotional hurts held in our mind. It progresses to become physical through our ongoing resistance to it.

Becomes physical ... you mean disease?

Yes. It's not the day-to-day experiences in life that cause suffering. *It is our ongoing resistance that causes our disharmony and suffering.* If we didn't judge or reject our experiences, the experience simply flows through to completion and disharmony and suffering ends.

Lily, I know you are a logical person, so let me put this into an equation I call the suffering equation.

Suffering = Experience * Resistance [R]

What does it mean?

Suffering is born from the resistance we have to our experiences. For suffering to exist, it requires both an experience and resistance to it. If either of the elements on the right side of the equation are not there (zero), then suffering is not born.

Life is full of experiences. On their own, experiences are just experiences. Take resistance out of the picture, and all you have is experience. In short, **our suffering is born from resistance itself, suffering is never born from our experience.** [R]

You can have a beautiful experience, where you do not resist the experience, and it completes without any disharmony. The same is also true where you have a so-called 'painful' experience. You can have a painful experience, where you don't resist, and it completes without any ongoing disharmony or suffering. If you are with the experience completely without resistance, a 'painful' experience can also be very beautiful.

A painful experience can be beautiful?

I know this sounds odd, but it is true with regards to anything you don't resist. I know this because I have experienced hurtful situations in this way many times. When I allow and meet the experience, I've found it turns from pain to something quite beautiful. Of course there may be some initial discomfort, but as you allow instead of resist, the discomfort dissolves.

I don't believe you. How could this happen?

It is hard to explain how or why this happens, it is part of the way the universe works, so I suggest you experiment with it and you will find out for yourself.

It is in our trying to escape, in our avoidance or our denial that we keep the past alive. These experiences live on within us, alive, unexpressed and incomplete. Life, as it relates to us through our experiences, is always looking for expression and completion – striving for balance and harmony in an environment that is ever changing.

~ 4 ~

The perfect storm

But Steven, what about me? What does this stupid resistance have to do with me and my cancer?

I have been where you are and learned that there is a very effective way to meet and bring harmony to any challenge that life brings our way. To understand how this relates to you directly, it is best that I share my real life story. So let me rewind a little and share what happened.

That is why I called you. Tell me how you beat cancer.

Ok then. After the fifth grade my life continued much along the same path. I kept the pact with myself that I'd never ever feel those hurts again. This approach of burying things seemed to work, so I used it with just about everything in my life that I didn't want, from that point forward. My family situation continued to be challenging and at times a nightmare. My father was avoiding the situation that he wanted to rectify but didn't know how. He turned to drinking and also became alcoholic. My parents started feeding off each other, often taking turns getting drunk or being sober, and as a result they started fighting with each other. There was stability in the fact that I had a mother and father and a nice house and lived in a good community, however there was instability in the dysfunction happening at home. I would arrive home from school not really knowing what I was going to walk into. I resisted every painful situation I faced, burying it within, never to be felt again.

But of course I did feel it even through I didn't want to acknowledge it. On the outside I looked normal, but on the inside I was fighting these ill feelings that kept rising within me.

Growing up in this environment, I dreamed of having my own happy family. By the age of 35, Angelina and I were married with a house, two children and a dog named Sparkey.

After starting my own software consultancy, I was making good money and we were paying off our mortgage at a steady rate. Around eight years into running my company things were growing strongly. I had just completed a successful two-year contract with the state government and we had some money in the bank. The kids were at a good age, walking, talking but not in school yet and I thought it would be a great time for a trip to America to share them with my parents and brothers. Angelina and I had been living in Australia since we got married, and my family in Boston had not spent any time with my kids, so we planned a six-month stay in Boston.

As luck would have it, I scored a software contract with a large insurance company in Boston to support this trip. We booked our flights and rented a little townhouse halfway between my parent's house and my work in downtown Boston.

Upon our arrival in Boston, we spent the first week at my

parent's house, the house I grew up in. A traditional New England three-story A-frame house made of wood and cedar in the wooded suburbs outside of Boston. It was autumn and the leaves were a bright combination of yellow, orange and red falling from their branches as the kids tried to catch them. The weather was cool but not snowing yet. The kids really enjoyed running around my parents' one-acre property, experiencing nature from the other side of the world. They rolled in the leaves and chased the squirrels who were madly trying to collect as many nuts as they could in preparation for the cold winter months ahead. It was great to see Cameron and Julia thriving in the loving attention they received from their grandparents and just about everyone who heard their unusual Australian accents. My parents seemed very happy to have us there, and they adored meeting and spending time with their grandkids. Those first days in Boston were some of the happiest of my life. One big happy family!

My work at the insurance company started straight away. I had negotiated a good contract so the money was rolling in and everything seemed to be working out perfectly.

Finishing my first week on the job, I took the train back from the city to my parents' house really looking forward to seeing everyone, especially Angelina, as that special spark between us had returned.

As I walked into my parents' house I sensed something strange, yet familiar. It was the same feeling I had when I was a child growing up in this house. My parents turned away from me as I walked into the living room and I heard a crying sound coming from downstairs. I ran downstairs and found Angelina, her face red, tears pouring out of her eyes. She turned and looked at me and started screaming at me. She was so upset I couldn't understand what she was saying.

I tried to calm her down and then made out what she had been saying "I want to go home. I am getting out of this fucking house and I am NEVER coming back here ever again!"

Stunned, I asked "what happened?"

She screamed: "Your mother is a fucking bitch! How dare you take me to this place. I am leaving and never coming back!"

I was in shock and didn't know what to say or do. I just sat there looking at her, frozen in disbelief. I tried to speak but couldn't. All the muscles in my body tensed up just like when I was younger when confronted with an emotional situation I didn't want. Angelina continued her tirade, now directed at me because I was standing there frozen in front of her. She didn't know my worst nightmare was coming true.

As she continued crying and screaming, I finally snapped out of it enough to realise where I was. I then reacted the way I always did in this house, I got her and the kids in the car and we ran away from what was happening.

I thought she was just upset, that it was like a bad storm that would blow over. The next day she was calmer, but still very angry and she made it perfectly clear that there was NO WAY she was ever going back to my mother's house or would ever see her again.

What happened between them?

They had a nasty verbal fight. I am not exactly sure what was said, as each of them have their own story about it. Angelina and I had done a lot of work to pack up our house and life in Australia to come visit my parents in America. My mother likely said something that sparked the fight off, with Angelina feeling rejected and insulted despite the hard work and sacrifices she made to get us all to America. Whatever was said, it must have touched a deep nerve because Angelina didn't take it quietly, she defended herself by attacking. Each of them using words that went straight for the jugular, more permanent than if they had fought with fists and nails.

It is likely that in my mother's eyes, Angelina is the woman who 'stole her son away' to the other side of the world. So that may have been the fuel that sparked it off.

So here I was back in the place I grew up, in the same situation I had lived in as a child. Now stuck in the middle of the two most important women in my life and trying to make it 'all right' for everyone. I was thrust back into a role I took on from a young age; I became the family saviour and peace-maker, desperately trying to hold the family together. My mother and Angelina were pulling at me from opposite directions, both trying to get my allegiance. I was forced into a situation of choosing between my mother and my wife.

As the days passed, I became furious, wondering why the fuck everyone couldn't just get along. All I ever wanted was to bring my new family to my parents so that everyone could be happy together. Secretly, I became angry that nobody cared about how important this was to me. All they wanted was to have a stupid fight and destroy everything.

Trying to ignore my anger I threw myself into work. On the weekends the kids and I spent time with my parents without Angelina who refused to go back to my parent's house. At first I asked and then begged her to join us, but she remained rigid and refused. For the entire six months in Boston, she never returned to my parent's house or attended any family event where my mother was present. This gutted me.

As each week went by my frustration towards Angelina's stand turned into raw anger, like an active volcano that I kept a lid on. Day by day, I felt more alienated from her and soon we began our own verbal fights. I felt betrayed and abandoned by her while at the same time feeling like I was the one being punished for a fight between the two women in my life. This was the story I told myself, that I was a victim who had been betrayed and abandoned and I pointed my fingers of blame squarely at both of them.

I wanted to let them have it, and let rip for their selfish petty behaviour. But I wouldn't let myself do that, because I was still trying to save the situation, still asking Angelina to come with me to visit my family, still hanging onto the dream of one happy family. So as I had done all my life, I just bottled my emotions up inside and pretended everything was ok. But my rage was so raw and explosive I could barely contain it.

The symptoms started soon after the incident at my parent's house. My stomach became unsettled, bloated, puffed out and at the same time it bubbled and gurgled. I ignored the symptoms and wrote it off as too many beers and hot dogs with my brother on the weekend. As these symptoms became worse over the six months in Boston, I was forced to take antacid tablets daily to try and subdue my stomach pains.

We left America six months later, leaving my dream behind in a train wreck that split me down the middle between the two most important women in my life.

Soon after we returned to Australia, we planned a trip to the countryside to take the kids to see their Australian Grandparents who lived on a five-hundred acre farm. It was a beautiful place with lots of farm animals and plenty of open land for the kids to explore.

As we got into the car to go to the farm I said to Angelina "Please don't tell your parents about the fight you had with my mother in America, it won't help matters and your mother will just take it out on me".

Angelina said "OK" and we drove off to the farm.

My mother in-law Anna is from Salerno Italy and my father in-law George is from the island of Kefalonia in Greece. It was a very European farmhouse with the main meal of the day served precisely at twelve noon. Anna is an amazing cook and she always treated us to a beautiful Italian meal that had been slow cooked on an old wood burning stove.

Anna is a tiny thing, less than five foot tall and skinny as a rail, but she is an incredibly strong women, one who grew up on a farm in Salerno during the German occupation of World War II. She lived through incredible adversity, caught right in the middle of the war during her teenage years. Food was scarce and she had to bury soldiers who had been killed near their farm. Like my mother, Anna was a real survivor who eventually left Italy to come to live in Australia. A few years earlier Anna had survived breast cancer even after the doctors gave her only three months to live. She was tough all right, and she had a memory that never forgets when somebody wronged her. I had somehow managed to stay on her good side all of these years and I never wanted to be on her bad side.

It was great to be back on the farm. Angelina's father George had been cooking a lamb on the open spit-fire all morning, the Greek way. He was taking the lamb off the flames when we arrived. We celebrated and had a wonderful three-hour lunch of home grown lamb, vegetables, and home made wine.

In the afternoon of the next day, I drove off to visit my friend Jim who lived in the same town as Anna and George. Jim and I watched the football game as we enjoyed a couple of cold beers. After sunset, I drove back to the farm.

As I parked my car and walked toward the front door, I heard Angelina talking in a loud animated way but I couldn't make out what she was saying from outside. Curious as to what the excitement was, I stood still for a moment and listened. I heard her say "And then Steven's Mom called me a fucking ...". My heart sank.

I couldn't believe she was telling her parents about the fight in America after she had promised me she wouldn't. I burst through the door saying "What are you doing, why are you doing this? You promised!" Angelina yelled back "I have the right to tell my mother what happened to me over there. How dare you tell me I can't tell her this!"

I took a step back in shock. I thought I had left this nightmare behind on the other side of the world. Like a virus lying dormant in my body, it activated itself in my safe haven of Australia. Yes, whatever we resist persists, only postponed to a future day. And it gets stronger and louder the longer we put it off. I just stood there stunned.

What did you do?

How could I defend myself? Everyone in the room was looking at me as if I was the guilty one. I hadn't done anything, but all fingers were being pointed at me. I was only trying to keep the peace, trying to save the situation. All I'd ever wanted was to share my kids and my family in America, but life had a different idea.

Anna looked at me and said "How dare you! She has the right to get this off her chest".

With disgust, I glared at Angelina and then walked out and went to bed.

As I lay in bed, I felt so hurt with everything spinning out of control. I had been betrayed and abandoned yet again. Now I was stuck smack in the middle of the three most important women in my life, with no way to escape the situation. There was no way out.

Tossing and turning all night I kept replaying what happened. I woke well before sunrise feeling emotionally exhausted. I walked into the living room and saw Anna in the kitchen stoking the wood-burning stove. As I entered the kitchen to say good morning, she stood up, turned, looked at me coldly and said: "What are you still doing here?"

I felt a wall of negativity hit me, engulfed by a force that pushed me away. Shocked, I turned and walked away. But there was nowhere to escape to in this small farmhouse. So I sat on a dusty chair in the storage room that was filled with old cardboard boxes and musty blankets covered in cobwebs as I waited for the kids to wake up. My stomach tightened and then started bubbling as it did in Boston. Not being able to sit still, I woke the kids up, loaded the car and we got the hell out of there.

In the following days back at my house in Sydney, my mind was spinning out, replaying the events over and over again like a broken record. I felt hurt and betrayed and started experiencing cramps and pains in my lower belly. My stomach became bloated, but this time much more pronounced than it was in America. I found having a bowel movement difficult as my stomach was tied in knots. Within a couple weeks I noticed blood in my stool which I ignored. Ignoring what I didn't want to see had become my normal response. Then it came – the tap on the shoulder that changed everything.

~ 5 ~

Disharmony is just
a call for inquiry

This tap on the shoulder was a rap from the universe itself. Sometimes it takes a very firm tap to get our attention, so that we bypass our habit of avoidance for just a moment, sit up, take notice and begin to see what we closed our eyes to.

The spontaneous healing of my cancer showed me what is possible when we have the courage to allow and be with whatever we are resisting.

> I have been fighting anxiety for the past ten years and feel on edge most of the time. I haven't told many people about my anxiety because I don't know what the anxiety is and I'm afraid to find out.

Lily, you are not alone. Anxiety is very common these days. Being aware of the anxiety and acknowledging it is a huge first step towards dissolving it. You described the situation perfectly in saying that you don't know what is behind the anxiety and are scared to find out. It is the nature of resistance that we are often unaware of what we are resisting. What are we all so scared of? *We are afraid of what we don't know. We are afraid of the unknown, those invisible inner things we have been running from for so long.* It is this fear of the unknown that keeps us running and in resistance, and sometimes it takes a tap on the shoulder, a situation we can't avoid like a life threatening illness, which gives us the courage to become curious and investigate.

You can't be telling me that cancer is a good thing?

I try not to judge any situation as good or bad. The reality is that cancer is here and it is tapping your shoulder. Do we continue the ways of the past that led to this situation, or do we stop, look and become aware of what is behind it? Cancer asks you this question in no uncertain terms.

But cancer can kill me!

Cancer is an extremely confronting situation and this tap on the shoulder is direct and to the point, but you would be surprised how the majority of people in this situation will still look the other way and ignore the wake up call.

Sometimes the message has to be very strong and to the point for us not to ignore it. For me it was the only way I would 'get it' after thirty years of continually looking the other way. For me, being confronted with death was a hidden blessing. It was the only way I was going to stop, look and uncover what I had been avoiding all my life. I talk to a lot of people who have had cancer and other diseases, and many of them say that the disease was a 'gift' marking the beginning of their 'real' life.

When I got the tap on the shoulder I was extremely scared. Afraid of death and the unknown, I had no idea why at the age of 38 cancer was here. Even with the dramatic family events that took place right before the symptoms of cancer appearing, I didn't connect the dots to anything in my past. Instead I went into shock and then reacted like most people do when they are first diagnosed, looking for a way out, a way to kill the cancer. In other words, I reacted automatically with resistance.

But my doctor talks about getting rid of cancer by killing it with chemotherapy. Shouldn't we kill cancer?

Cancer is the messenger and it's best not to shoot that messenger. Instead of resisting and wanting to 'kill cancer,' if we stop for a moment and listen to what the diagnosis is saying, we will see that the symptoms which doctors call cancer is pointing to something else, and that something else is what led to this situation called cancer.

Now would be a good time for you to become curious as to what led to cancer appearing and to investigate. And as part of your investigation it is good to explore 'the stories of me'.

Stories of me?

Yes, 'the stories of me' are the stories of our life we attach to our self. So take a look at your life from childhood to now, and review the stories that have stayed with you, the stories you continue to tell yourself and believe to be true. As you review your life, you may see a common thread running through it. You may find a theme that repeats throughout your life linked with certain experiences that seem to happen over and over again. 'The stories of me' are the stories we tell ourselves about ourselves in relation to others and our past experiences. As the common experiences repeat through life, this 'story of me' gets confirmed and becomes solidified. As our story becomes rigid, we also become more rigid. We believe the 'story of me' to be true and we hold onto this belief strongly and close our eyes to other possibilities. These stories and beliefs make up who we are, and unknowingly we will do just about anything to defend who we think we are and the stories that support this. In other words, these 'stories of me' can be what is behind our biggest resistance in life, and often it is here where we get stuck, where we would rather 'be right' in our definition of self than be in harmony.

How does this relate to my cancer?

Behind the situation you find yourself in is most likely a story and some beliefs that are unknowingly being harboured. So I simply encourage you to become curious and investigate, because seeing and acknowledging these stories that we hold onto so tightly, can be very helpful in healing what is behind your cancer situation.

What about you, what was your 'story of me'?

Well, the 'story of me' played out throughout my life and it played out again just before my cancer situation appeared. My 'story of me' is a story of being emotionally abandoned and betrayed, a victim to the women in my life. That story first played out with my mother, then with girlfriends, until I got married. Then that story played out with my wife during my marriage. The final straw came when the same story played out simultaneously with my wife, mother and mother in-law and the cancer appeared.

But why do you call it a 'Story of Me?' What is the 'Me'?

It's called the 'Story of Me,' because we become the story that we tell ourselves. We create a sense of self, a 'Me' around the very stories we make up in our mind and believe to be true. It is human nature that anything we truly believe, we will defend, even if it kills us! This is why cancer can be so challenging. Cancer, like any life threatening illness, asks us to become less rigid, to open and look at the very things we are defending at all costs; 'me and my stories'. Yes, we are very attached to our stories and the beliefs connected to them, because they are the elements that we define as 'me'.

I encourage you to use the situation of cancer as an excuse to investigate, to temporarily let down your defences, and become aware of and explore your stories and related beliefs. In this open stance you may see things from a new perspective. Also, I suggest you review the emotional experiences that happened in the months just prior to cancer appearing. As with my case, these experiences leave clues to the stories and beliefs you are harbouring and the emotional theme that may be linked with your cancer.

So how did this help you beat cancer?

Well, after returning from my in-laws' farm, I had physical

symptoms in my lower stomach and then blood appeared in my stool. I just ignored it hoping it would go away. But in the days to come, the symptoms got worse and so I went to see my family doctor who scheduled me for a colonoscopy, where they would use a little camera to look inside.

But before the colonoscopy and the cancer diagnosis, a friend of mine told me about a special stomach doctor named Dr. V and she highly recommended I go see him. I went straight away and he quickly gave the diagnosis of 'Leaky Gut Syndrome'. His solution for this was a special program of herbs and Chinese medicine taken daily over a four month period. Looking for an easy way out, I gladly jumped on Dr. V's herbal program, which cost me about $100 per day. Towards the end of my first meeting with Dr. V. I told him that I had already been scheduled for a colonoscopy for the following week. He told me to cancel the colonoscopy, he was sure that at the age of 38, I had 'Leaky Gut Syndrome'.

So I cancelled the colonoscopy and followed Dr. V's program religiously which also included a special diet of no meat, dairy, wheat or alcohol. Over the next three months of following this program, my symptoms got worse. Sharing my condition with Dr. V. in our regular meetings, he told me to stay with his program. Finally, four months into the program after losing 11 kilos (24 pounds) in weight, Dr V said: "I think you better go get that colonoscopy ..."

Even though a part of me knew something was seriously wrong, my habit of ignoring what I didn't want to see, feel or experience, kept me in state of denial that I had a major problem. Up to this point cancer never crossed my mind as a possibility, so I had Dr. V. book me in for a colonoscopy.

Within a few days I had a colonoscopy and the doctor found a growth in my large intestine and took a biopsy. I remember when Angelina was driving me home, I felt a strange relief that they had found something. My only thought was that they needed to find something so they could deal with it. Even at this point cancer never crossed my mind.

Later that afternoon I drove to Dr. V's office to get the results of the biopsy. Coldly, he told me I had an advanced form of bowel cancer located in the large intestine and that they wanted to operate immediately. He scheduled me in for an emergency operation in five days time with a leading Sydney surgeon.

I couldn't believe my ears. Even being in the same room and hearing it come out of Dr. V's mouth, I felt like it wasn't really happening, and that it was all a bad dream. Dr. V. handed me an envelope with paperwork and other details to prepare for the operation. As I walked out of his office I realised it wasn't a dream.

Driving home from his office, emotions overwhelmed me. The drawbridge near my house opened up just as I was approaching it and I was forced to stop and be still. I looked in the rear view mirror seeing my own eyes peering back at me. Looking deep within myself I saw what I had never seen before: sadness, fear and emptiness, as tears rolled down my face. For the first time in my life I was staring death in the face.

Arriving home I pulled myself together and put on a brave face for Angelina. She came out of the house to greet me and as I told her the news she collapsed to the ground. She became so sick with fear she could barely get off the couch for days.

We didn't tell the kids what was going on, we just said that mommy was not feeling well and daddy was going to have an operation.

Waves of fear hit me regularly. To deal with it, I would sneak upstairs into the shower where I would cry hysterically.

I had hidden my emotions throughout my life but I couldn't bury this. These emotions were uncontrollable – pure, raw and un-adulterated and they hit me like a runaway locomotive.

But there it was, the tap on the shoulder. Cancer was asking me to stop running away and become real. It was telling me I was ready. You don't get the tap on the shoulder unless you are ready.

With a little shift in awareness we can ask ourselves: Is cancer the enemy or is cancer here with a greater message? Did cancer appear out of thin air or is it the result of something? Am I a victim or a participant in what is happening? Can I give this situation away to someone else to deal with or am I responsible for what I call my life?

Lily, with a little shift, you may be able to see that cancer is a symptom and not the cause of the situation you are facing. So, what to do? Kill the symptom or look beneath the symptom to uncover and heal what caused it to be here?

Are you telling me not to get rid of cancer?

No, not at all. Deal with the immediate emergency and look to the underlying cause of your symptom to heal it forever. *The solution to cancer or any disharmony lies in the cause, not the symptom, and any form of disharmony is a signal for you to inquire within.*

~ 6 ~

Don't fight it, invite it

Did you find the cause of your cancer?

Yes.

How did you do it?

It was part of what unfolded next. It was five days before my operation and some very interesting things happened. For the first time I pondered life and death, and asked myself some very direct questions related to death and dying. I wondered if I was happy with what I had accomplished in this life or if I made a difference to anyone? Had I been a good and honourable man? Would I be remembered by anyone in any particular way? The answers that came were not as I had hoped. I had had a somewhat wild time for a large portion of my life, partying a lot from my teenage years up until the age of thirty. In my thirties I had a young family that I loved deeply, and this was my greatest achievement from what I saw. The truth was that my focus had been mainly on myself with a primary focus on achieving success from a material and personal perspective. My answer was no, I had not really made a difference that I was aware of, and I didn't feel fulfilled or happy with myself or my accomplishments if I was to suddenly leave the planet.

What stuck out the most from my inquiry was my children. I didn't want to leave my kids. More than anything, I wanted to be here for them, to guide and support them, to love them and to help shape them into beautiful happy people. I wanted them to have a happy and loving home with a mother and father. Visions of my kids growing up without a father tore at my heart. Then a very strange thing happened.

It was the morning of the third day after my diagnosis. I was in the shower, the special place that I felt safe enough to let go and allow my emotions to flow. With the hot water running on the back of my neck, my emotions erupted. My body convulsed, the tears flowed from my eyes, and a sad scream came out from the back of my throat. For some reason I just let it happen and didn't fight it.

Suddenly the screaming stopped as if an invisible vacuum sucked all the fear, sorrow and self-pity out of me. It was gone and I came into a unexpected state of calmness. I just stood there for a while remaining still, quietly observing the situation at hand. For the first time since the diagnosis, I fully accepted the real possibility of my own death. I said to myself "OK, I could die." With this statement I let go and accepted the situation as it was and no longer fought with the reality that was here. As this happened, a question came to me out of the blue. It appeared within my mind like a neon sign and I needed to answer this question right then and there. That question was:

Am I going to be a victim and die OR am I going to Live?

Without hesitation my answer shot back loud and clear.

"THERE IS NO FUCKING WAY I AM GOING TO DIE AND NOT BE WITH MY KIDS GROWING UP, NO FUCKING WAY!"

Surprised by the question, I was equally surprised at the power and clarity of my answer. That was it, the decision was made, and with that decision nothing, I mean not a thing was going to stop me.

Where did the question come from?

I can't really say exactly where the question came from. However, looking back I see that I had hit a critical point I call the 'Decision Point'. The Decision Point is a moment people come to when threatened with their own mortality. It is a moment of truth where we make a choice.

Of course, when some people reach this point they can still run away from making a decision hoping the situation will just go away. Many people take on the stance of a victim, bow their head, and relinquish their responsibilities to others to save them. You can also choose life and let your decision be known. It is really up to you. Making no decision is like being a fish out of water, the universe isn't clear of your intention, and you can run out of breath.

What do you mean the universe isn't clear of your intention?

You know, this existence, this universe, life itself, this mysterious source of life that empowers your body to breathe in and breathe out. There are many ways to name the great power, the life force that created us and is behind us, I just call it the universe.

One way we interact with the universe is through our intention, so it is important to be clear what our intention is in relation to cancer. *The universe reflects back to us what we intend, what we believe and what we expect.* Intention is the spark that kick-starts what is manifested in life. Intention is the quiet yet potent communication you can initiate with the universe and its greater intelligence.

In my case, my intention was very clear. Powered by the unconditional love for my children, I spoke assertively and clearly so there was NO WAY the universe could misinterpret me. Looking upwards in the shower, I said again:

"THERE IS NO FUCKING WAY I AM GOING TO LEAVE THIS PLANET AND NOT BE WITH MY KIDS GROWING UP"

This was a turning point.

Does the Decision Point come to all of us?

Everyone I have met who has had the tap has come to this Decision Point knowingly or unknowingly. Some people 'get it' like in my case and the question appears in a way that they respond to it. Others ignore it leaving their intended path unclear.

For example, I have an interesting friend named Neville whose response was even louder than mine.

Neville had become ill after his wife demanded a divorce and he discovered that she had cheated on him with another man. He underwent a number of medical tests and his doctor told him "Neville, you have bowel and testicular cancer. You only have three months to live". Hearing this, Neville stood up in front of the doctor's desk, looked the doctor straight in the eyes, raised his clenched fists high in the air and screamed out an emphatic, "NO!" as he slammed his fists down on the doctors desk, literally breaking the desk into two.

This was Neville's Decision Point and he found his own way to let the universe know what his intentions were. He didn't buy into the three-month death sentence. He didn't turn over his power to his doctor.

He didn't believe the doctor?

No. It is interesting isn't it. The doctor knew nothing about Neville, nothing about his character, his intent, his will to live and purpose to remain alive. The doctor knew nothing about Neville's past, or his strength of mind and psyche. The doctor only responded from what he knew and this response was based on his university training, his past experiences using conventional cancer treatments and the bag of statistics that comes with the job. The doctor reached into this to come up with his death sentence. Lily, we are not 'statistics', each of us are unique human beings. The doctor was only looking at a symptom in the body, and wasn't considering the power of the person's spirit. The typical medical doctor is not trained to investigate these things, nor does he have the time to uncover the 'real' person he is treating.

These events with Neville took place over twenty years ago. Neville recently got married to the love of his life and is stronger than ever, one hundred percent cured of cancer.

The Decision Point is a moment of choice. If we give responsibility to someone else to make the decision for us, we relinquish our choice. When we relinquish our choice, then our destiny is in the hands of others whose desires, motives, intent, beliefs and view of the world might not be in line with our own. In not making a choice we can end up in no man's land, a vast open plane of confusion where we send mixed messages to the universe. As we are unclear, the universe will be equally unclear and reflect this back to us in our physical life. There are no right or wrong decisions, but it is important to make a decision.

Our reality follows our beliefs. If Neville had relinquished his power to the doctor, the 'man of authority' in the white jacket, if Neville had taken on the belief that he had three months to live, Neville's story would likely have been much different than it turned out to be.

But everyone is telling me what to do!

What Neville shows and what I suggest is to believe in and follow yourself, to follow what feels right to you. *You are the best person to know what is right for you.* Yes, many people are telling you what to do, but they don't live inside your skin, only you will know what is right for you. The answers are within you Lily. I hope to show you how to get in touch with this wisdom within yourself.

With those clear words in the shower that morning, my will was strong, my intent clear and my purpose focused and unshakable. I chose life!

How did that happen, I mean you were crying hysterically in
the shower?

What enabled this to transpire is an awareness, a state of presence
that allowed me to move out of a hysterical state of my mind, a
mind that was in resistance to cancer and death, to become still and
accept whatever was there in the moment.

How did that happen?

To be honest, at the time I didn't know what was happening. This
calm accepting awareness came like a flash flood that filled me.
What happened in the shower is that I realised I was dying. This was
enough for me to stop resisting the situation I was in. With resistance
no longer there, awareness came flooding in, and instantly my state
shifted from being hysterical and resistant, to being present, aware
and accepting of what was there in that moment.

Facing death and accepting that I was dying shot me out of
identifying with my mind and its endless stories and fears. As a
result, resistance stopped, the stories stopped and the need to
escape the situation called cancer stopped. All those things that
stopped were part of the mind and its workings. Awareness awaits
beyond the mind, and I became instantly calm and present in a
state of awareness.

This is one of the benefits to a life-threatening situation, as it
often brings you into focus, into a new state of awareness. And in a
new state of awareness, everything including your health changes.

A new state of awareness?

Awareness is an inner state where you are calm and present to what is happening in and around you in that moment. With awareness, you become an impartial witness to whatever is happening, just observing things as they are. It is here that you tap into the answers meant for you.

I don't know about this ... You think this is right for me?

It is certainly a great place to start. There is an intelligence that is all around you and inside of you. No two people are the same, each have their own path, their own right way. Being present, being here now with what is happening will certainly help the mind become quiet and allow the intelligence that is ever present to find the right path for you.

Many people diagnosed with a life threatening illness fall into panic and fear because they are focused on the future, or stuck in the past. Awareness exists only in the moment, never in the past or the future. The here and now is your inner compass and guide.

How do you know this?

It was part of what I learned by experiencing it. Strangely, it came through surrendering to…or should I say accepting that moment. In the shower that day I accepted death. I accepted the real fact that I might die. For the three days prior, I was in complete and utter chaos and denial, an emotional wreck fighting death and not taking responsibility for anything. Internally, I took no responsibility for my physical condition and I was caught in story, blaming the women in my life, blaming Dr. V., pointing the finger at everything outside of myself, looking at myself as a victim. In those three days leading up to that fateful day in the shower, I was fighting the whole idea of death in the only way I knew how, by resisting it.

It's crazy how in those three days following my diagnosis, I spent most of my time preparing for a legal battle against Dr. V. because he wrongly diagnosed my health situation as 'Leaky Gut Syndrome' and put me on a herbal program that delayed my colonoscopy by four months and allowed the cancer to advance. In resistance I put my focus on the future, a future for my wife and kids where they could be looked after, obtain some money from a law suit against Dr. V. I actually sat down and wrote out every detail about my interactions with Dr. V. that my wife would need for a law-suit against him if I didn't survive. This is typical of how resistance manifests. In this case it diverted my attention to the future instead of where it needed to be, which was there in that moment, with the situation called cancer.

So in the shower that morning I became real and accepted that I was dying. In meeting death, I switched outside the mind and its story, and all of the fighting, blaming and anger just dropped away in that instant.

What really stood out in this experience of surrendering to death and dying is that the fear around death and dying disappeared. The fear I had been experiencing up to this point vanished, I was no longer afraid to die.

But you didn't want to die, so why did you surrender to death?

Good question. I didn't surrender as in giving up. It was a different kind of surrendering. *Surrendering is simply a letting go of resistance, the avoidance of what is here. It is being aware and not looking for an escape route to avoid the situation.* Surrender is not a weakness it is a great strength. It is a letting go to allow what is here right now.

So I was not surrendering to 'dying', I was not saying: "I want to die." In surrendering, I accepted the situation instead of trying to escape it. In that letting go to what was here, I became present and the suffering I had been experiencing such as the fear of death, anxiety surrounding my stories, the need to fight what I didn't want to experience, they all dissolved.

As strange as it may sound, as I stepped out of the shower that day, I found myself in a state of peace and stillness. In this peaceful state, I was presented with two unexpected gifts.

The first gift was a laundry list of life's priorities that appeared within my mind. On the left were my old priorities, my life's focus up until this point. On the right were the new priorities, what 'really' mattered, based on truth that had been revealed from looking at the face of death with awareness.

Old Priorities	New True Priorities
Success, Career, Achievements Money Material Things Family Love	**Love** **Family** Health This very moment, now

In the face of death I could see that money had absolutely no meaning at all, and the material things that I owned meant nothing, zilch. My career, my titles, becoming someone successful – I saw how I spent most of my life chasing these false gods. What had been at the bottom of my old life priorities was now clearly at the top of my new priorities. I saw the simplicity of the truth that all that really mattered was Love, particularly the love of my family. I know this sounds a bit cliché, but this is what I saw. Love and my family stood out, followed by two new important things: health and this moment, now.

The second gift was the gift of presence that I have been talking about. In the afternoon of the same day, my kids returned home after an outing. We sat in the living room and got out the wooden blocks and played. I had played blocks with my kids many times in the past, but had never been totally present with them as I was this day. We poured the blocks onto the carpet, we read out the letters and numbers and built a little house and laughed as we knocked it over. No longer seeing life through the limiting filter of my mind, I found myself completely present with my kids and it was blissful. Every micro-second with them was pure bliss. I felt like the luckiest man on earth. Each second a gift, one that I appreciated for the first time. It was so simple and yet I had never seen it before. Being with my kids in this state was everything; it was worth more than anything I had ever owned. This is the gift of presence, and I came to understand what it means to be living in the moment, in the micro-second of time, in the now. Nothing in the past really mattered anymore, and the future didn't matter either because I might not have a future. All that mattered was this beautiful right-now.

It is amazing what is right in front of us all the time that we don't see. All the material things society tells us we should strive for to become fulfilled. The truth is that happiness can be found in the perfection of right now; not the past, not the future – right now. *What is behind us is just a reflection of what was, what is ahead of us is a projection of what might be. Right now is the only thing that is real.*

What a wonderful gift I received in just being with my kids and getting it! How simple, how beautiful. A heightened experience of unconditional love. This was bliss, a moment of heaven on earth that can only be experienced when you are present, fully here now.

~ 7 ~

You are the Awareness
behind the eyes

After that, what did you do to heal cancer?

The cancer was advanced, it was an emergency situation that I had to deal with, and that's what I did next.

So off to hospital I went. It was one of the older Sydney hospitals run by the government's health system. A very busy place, full of public patients most of whom rely on the government's free health service, Medicare.

I arrived and they directed me to the bowel ward. The nurse at that ward asked me to follow her to my room. Well it wasn't really my room, but an old waiting room they had converted to a shared bedroom. The room contained eight beds in two rows of four with little space between each bed. Seven of the beds were occupied by very old men who looked tired and lifeless. It felt like a morgue.

A few days earlier, my surgeon told me I would get a private room. I had anticipated having the night before the operation to myself, to psych myself up, to get mentally ready for this big event. Standing there in this living morgue, I felt myself shutdown like a computer that was unplugged from the wall.

I didn't go to my bed, instead I turned and walked down the hallway to a small TV room with a couple of 1960's vintage orange suede chairs and a small black and white TV. I sat there staring at the ground, wondering how I got here and what I was going to do. I just couldn't go back to that room. My will was being tested and I wasn't sure I could stay true to doing 'whatever it took' to survive.

Four hours later a nurse came through the door and stood in front of me with a beaming smile on her face. She told me that a patient had just been discharged and they now had a private room ready for me. Like a prayer being answered, I felt my body fill with energy as we walked to my room.

The room was old and somewhat unclean but it offered me solitude. I spent the rest of the afternoon and night preparing myself mentally. During my university days in finals exam week, I would motivate myself with music just before I took my exam. In the same spirit, I brought a few CD's to hospital to listen to before my operation. As I lay in bed the night before the operation, I reached in and pulled a random CD out of my bag. It happened to be a new unopened CD titled 'Made in Heaven' by the rock band Queen.

As I listened to the music, visions from childhood up to the present flashed in my mind as if I was witnessing an opera of my own life. Made in Heaven was created by the great Freddie Mercury, his last album before he died. It is a bit of a requiem; his statement to the world about life, love, and wanting to live. He was dying when he wrote this music and it mirrored where I was, at that exact moment, facing death and wanting to live. With my headphones on, Freddie spoke to me that night. It felt like he was in the room preparing me for what lay ahead. As the CD finished I fell into a deep restful sleep.

The next morning I woke ten minutes before I was scheduled to go in the operating theatre. I quickly put my headphones on to play one last song. I reached into my bag and pulled out the sound track to the movie Armageddon, and listened to a powerful rock ballad by Arrowsmith's Steve Tyler called "I don't want to miss a thing." It was such an appropriate song as I faced my own Armageddon. I played it loud and psyched myself up for what was about to happen. My whole body vibrated to the message held in the music's frequencies. "I don't want to close my eyes, don't want to go to sleep, because I'll miss you babe, and I don't want to miss a thing ..." A single tear rolled down my cheek as the nurses came in and wheeled me away. I was as ready as I would ever be.

The operation lasted four hours. I awoke in the recovery room with Angelina by my side. I took one look at her and tears started flowing as I fell instantly back to sleep.

Some hours later I awoke and was back in my room. I remember being a bit agitated which is a typical side effect of the anaesthetic that was still flowing through my body. For some reason my right eye was bothering me, there was something in my eye. It was so annoying and I let the nurses know about it. The doctors were in the hall and within seconds there were four doctors poking around in my eye trying to fix it. They started using tweezers and gauze on my eye and it all became far too complicated. Finally I just burst out loud and shouted to Angelina "Go down to the hospital store and get me some fucking eye drops". She returned with the goods and with two droplets, the problem was solved. I was definitely still alive.

I spent most of the next couple of days sleeping. My body so naturally intelligent, knew exactly what to do at this moment. It shut down parts of the body to focus the energy resources to the areas that need it the most. *The human body is a Healing Machine.*

The third day after the operation I no longer needed to sleep all day, I was awake most of the day. On that day I felt different, like a new person. It was as if my eyes were new, getting used to seeing for the first time. Everything seemed more alive, more illuminated and had new meaning. I was alive, but not the same person I had been, as if an old part of me died and a new part of me was born.

What part of you died?

What died was that aspect of me that said 'No' to life. That part of me that was always staying super busy as a means of running away from my inner hurts. That part of me that was just going through the motions day by day, focused on career and money, always striving for success.

What was it?

Most people call it the Ego. The Ego is the part of me that says 'No' to life. After the operation it was no longer in the driver's seat. Before the operation I saw the old and new laundry list of life's priorities. After the operation, my entire being shifted to the right side of that laundry list. I woke up from the operation with a new focus towards Love, Family, Health and 'This very moment'. I was no longer attracted to the things the Ego focuses on to inflate and sustain itself, such as personal status, money, material things, being stuck in the past, worrying about the future and avoiding what is here now.

Ok, so what new part of you was born?

The authentic me. It was not really born, but uncovered, because it was always there. When the authentic you is uncovered you feel alive and new, like something has been born.

Authentic me? What are you talking about?

Many interesting things happened on the third day after the operation as my energy returned. I started to experience myself as two beings, two separate entities that were entwined together. There was this physical me, which was a body, and it was experiencing this intense pain. Then there was the other me, the 'real' me that was not the body, that was simply witnessing the body and the intense pain. Throughout my life I had always thought of myself as this body, but in hospital at this time it became very clear that the 'real' me was not the body at all.

So I lay there in bed all day long and the real me was simply witnessing everything that was happening in and around this body, which was no longer the real me. It was a strange experience to suddenly see that I was not my body. I really didn't understand what was going on. I was stuck in bed for ten days not allowed to get up, so all I could do was continue to witness this.

It was the fourth day in hospital when it happened … what I can only describe as the cells of my body speaking to me. Words came clearly to me, but there was nobody else in the room. And these words didn't come from outside of me, they came from inside, not from my head, but from all places in my body in unison.

Your cells spoke? Lily asked incredulously.

Yes, that's the best way to describe it. The cells explained the experience I was having in which I witnessed the body as something other than me. The words that came were "*You are the Awareness behind the eyes.*" This awareness behind the eyes that I am, was calmly witnessing all the events unfolding around me. Lying there in my hospital bed, I just observed, going with the flow of whatever occurred, aware yet unconcerned.

How did the cells speak? Did you hear words?

No, not words, it was a communication that was happening inside me, like a direct signal to my brain which interpreted the message. The communication was very clear and distinct. I only received a few direct messages, but each message was very important. As a result I started to feel more comfortable with the experience that was happening in hospital.

Why were you more comfortable?

I think it is because I came to know that I was not the object of what was happening, I was the thing that was witnessing it all. For example, a nurse came in every couple of hours to inject me with a needle. After receiving the message from my cells, I just calmly observed the nurse sticking the needle into the body. Taking the needle was no longer of concern, as I knew that the body wasn't the real me, but more like a vehicle for the real me.

Sitting in my bed day after day the nurses came and went, and although I was feeling a lot of physical pain, I was mainly peaceful. In hospital I came to see that I am not this body, I am something my cells called awareness, and I experienced an infinite calmness just observing it all. Although surreal, it was very REAL.

Then my cells spoke again in an experience I call 'the Knowing'.

The Knowing?

It was an experience that was unlike any other. What happened was I suddenly 'knew', without any shadow of doubt or any possibility of being wrong, that I was going to survive this cancer emergency.

How did you know?

The cells spoke in one voice: "You will survive, but to live you must find out what caused the cancer". This knowing came as both a message and a feeling.

Are you sure you weren't imagining this?

Yes, I am sure. This knowing wasn't a belief, it wasn't something you would call blind faith and it surely wasn't a 'hope' that I would be OK. No, it was much more than that. This was the deepest, most profound knowing of truth that I have ever experienced. It was complete clarity of 'knowing,' and any remaining fear of death and self-doubt about survival vanished.

The voice of my cells was different from any voice I had ever heard before. It spoke from an infinite depth and the words resonated with the highest degree of integrity as if spoken from an all-loving authority. When I heard this voice, there was no mistaking its message as pure truth. This is why I call the experience 'the Knowing'. When you hear pure truth you know it.

You see, during the operation they had removed seventeen lymph nodes around my body. They sent them away to be tested, because the lymph nodes will show traces of cancer if the cancer had spread. Everyone around me was in a state of fear about getting these test results. The cancer was advanced and the doctors held fleeting hope for me. Angelina was a nervous wreck and was worried about my life, and our future. She came into my room every day filled with fear, anxiously wondering when we would get the results of the lymph node test. Nurses, doctors, friends and family brought their fears into my room during the following days, but the uncanny thing was I was impervious to their fear. It was like there was an invisible protective force field that surrounded my body, and other people's fear could not penetrate it to get to me.

How can this be?

I think what happened was that I was resonating in a higher state of 'knowing', and as a result, other people's doubts, fears, worries, concerns and negativity couldn't affect me.

Resonating, what do you mean?

In my positive state of knowing, I was immune to other people's negativity. The positive state is more powerful, a higher octave than the lower octave of fear, doubts and worries for example. So those lower negative states simply could not penetrate or affect me.

Were there any other messages from your cells?

No other messages, but what encompassed this entire experience at hospital was a pronounced feeling of gratitude. After the operation, I awoke feeling extremely grateful for everything that was happening. And that feeling didn't leave me.

Grateful for what? You had cancer!

Yes, I know it sounds strange, but there it was. Gratitude encircled my experience after waking up from the operation. I felt grateful for everything and everyone I had contact with. So unusual to be at the lowest point in my life, my physical body in the most pain I had ever experienced, and yet the inner me was so grateful. I really did feel like the luckiest guy on the planet.

Good drugs?

No, but I can see why you think that. I had an epidural to quell the pain. Gratitude had never been part of my life prior to this situation, but gratitude appeared and encompassed me. I believe this gratitude came about as part of a shift in consciousness that happened in the shower on the third day at home, and then around the time of the operation in hospital.

Shift in Consciousness?

Yes, a shift in my state of awareness. Our Consciousness is our state of awareness, and within this is our perceptions. How we perceive and experience life is based on our state of consciousness. My consciousness shifted and how I experienced my day-to-day reality went to a new place, a higher octave. This is why my sense of self suddenly shifted from being 'my body' to being 'the awareness behind the eyes', why I was seeing life through new eyes, why I was feeling grateful for everything and why fear and other negative emotions which used to be my constant companion were no longer part of me.

When your consciousness shifts, there is a fundamental change in how you see yourself and experience the world. Your sense of self, your very identity shifts. It is like a veil that has been covering your eyes is lifted. When the veil moves, you start to see things differently. Nothing is really different, but you perceive it from a new perspective.

I don't understand.

OK, let me step back a little. In our day-to-day lives we can be at various degrees of living unconsciously to living consciously. When living unconsciously, there is little awareness to each moment, we are more focused on the future and the past and often stuck in our lower emotions. When living unconsciously we tend to go through the motions day in and day out, like a machine on auto-pilot. When we live this way, we don't inspect what is happening in the moment. In fact we avoid any introspection. We are more concerned with our stories from the past and our fears of the future.

When living consciously, we live with awareness of things that are happening in the moment. It is the opposite of living in the past and the future. It is living here now. When something happens that provokes anger in you, you might respond with anger, but you also become aware of the anger, wonder what is behind it and inspect what the anger is about. Like an impartial witness, you see and feel what is happening. This is living with awareness, it is moment to moment, and through our observations, life reveals itself in a very real way.

Consciousness is a state of awareness, the awareness of being aware. Awareness is a state of witnessing, and by its very nature, it is present in each moment. Whereas unconsciousness is not aware, it is reactive, automatic and repetitive, and comes from that state which is focused on our past and our future, never here now. In short, **unconsciousness is the denial of experience.** [R]

So having a shift of consciousness simply means that I had a shift in my state of awareness, where I became present, saw things from a new perspective, a higher octave, and my old automatic habitual way of avoiding painful experiences had fallen away.

Why do you call it a higher octave?

You could say that consciousness has higher and lower levels, like the rungs on a tall ladder. At the lower levels, you are closer to the ground and have a limited perception of things. At the higher level, you have a broader vantage point, and thus see things differently. You see further away, you take in a wider view, there is more light on whatever you are looking at. And with this broader view of things, your perception of what you are looking at shifts. As your perception changes, everything about you and your life as you experience it changes.

Consciousness is hierarchical?

This is one way to interpret it, many levels of consciousness. Like a ladder, each rung has an associated level of awareness or perception with it. What I have learned through experiencing this shift is that where you are on this ladder relates directly to how you perceive things, how you interpret and respond to events and thus how you experience your day-to-day life. *Your level of consciousness becomes your experience, because your reality is based on the level of consciousness you are aligned with.* My consciousness shifted to a higher level, and even though I had cancer, I was experiencing gratitude, calmness, no fear and a knowing that I was going to survive.

Lily, there is a great book called *Power Vs. Force: The Hidden Determinates of Human Behaviour* by the renowned psychiatrist and doctor, Dr. David R. Hawkins which provides a map of Human Consciousness. Let me draw you an abstract of this Ladder of Human Consciousness as I remember it from that book.

Higher Consciousness

| Enlightenment |
| Peace |
| Joy |
| Love |
| Reason |
| Acceptance |
| Willingness |
| Neutrality |
| Courage |

Lower Consciousness

| Pride |
| Anger |
| Desire |
| Fear |
| Grief |
| Apathy |
| Guilt |
| Shame |

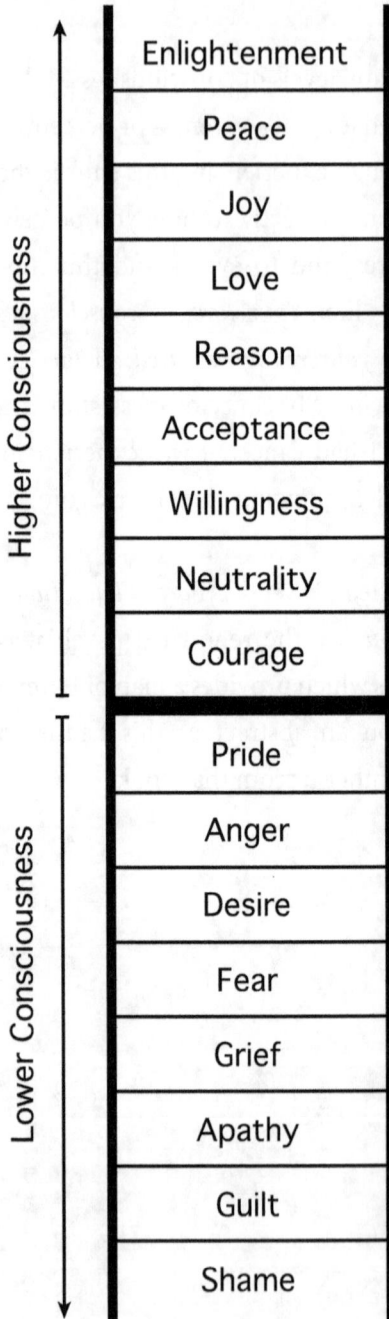

Source – *Power Vs. Force: The Hidden Determinates of Human Behaviour* – David R. Hawkins, M.D. PH.D

If aligned with the lower rungs of consciousness, you will likely experience life situations with various degrees of shame, guilt, fear or anger depending on where you are at. You can often get stuck in negativity and repetitive drama because resistance is a common characteristic associated with the lower levels of consciousness.

As your consciousness shifts upwards into the higher levels as with my experience, you will likely experience life situations with a greater degree of courage, acceptance and love. Your perception of things will expand and you will be more aware, open, and curious, naturally seeking out disturbances in your life like a conscientious gold miner discarding worthless pebbles while sifting for the gold.

So lower consciousness is bad and higher consciousness is good?

You see, this is a tricky one. As soon as we define one thing as bad and another thing as good, we move back into what we have been taught to do all of our life. To seek the 'good' and avoid the 'bad'. This judging is just the mind, namely the Ego that looks to stay in control through the means of separation. What I am trying to say here is that any level of consciousness is not 'good' or 'bad', it simply is consciousness. If you are experiencing a lot of anger in your life, this is a characteristic of a lower level of consciousness. Instead of looking at it as 'good' or 'bad', look at it like a road map or a thermometer, the feedback mechanism of life. If you are driving your car and suddenly your 'hot' light appears on the dashboard, it is telling you that your car is overheating and you should pull over, let the car rest, investigate and perhaps put cool water into your radiator. If you understand that consciousness is simply consciousness, and there is no goal in consciousness itself, you can use consciousness as a barometer. Cancer is one symptom. It is the body giving you feedback about your physical and mental state of health. When you become curious and look what's behind the reason the gauge on your dashboard is flashing 'cancer', you may find such things as anger, fear, guilt or shame for example. If you discover anger, that in itself is a signpost of where you are at. The signpost, like the 'hot' gauge in your car is suggesting that you become curious, pull over and investigate. To investigate, you don't need to obtain any special tools that are outside of yourself, you just move into presence with whatever is here. And through experiencing what is here, consciousness shifts and our life naturally changes to a new octave.

It is at the lower rungs of consciousness, where disharmony in any form is created and maintained. [R]

Is the opposite true? At the higher rungs is disharmony reversed?

You get it! There is a very special person in my life I haven't told you about yet, his name is Dr Rahasya Fritjof Kraft, someone I met soon after I left the hospital. He is the reason I am alive talking with you today. He is the one who pointed me to everything I am sharing with you, and who led me to my spontaneous cure. Before I tell you about him, let me answer your question the way Dr. Kraft explained it to me. In regards to the relationship between higher consciousness and healing, he said: *Where there is a shift of consciousness, spontaneous healing of anything can and often happens.* [R]

~ 8 ~

Ego is our resistance to What Is

You keep mentioning 'the Ego', what is it and why is it important?

It's important because the Ego is a sense of self of our own construction. It is an identity that we create and perpetuate. It is made up of the thoughts and beliefs about our self that we acquire over our lifetime. With these thoughts about our self that we agree with, we construct a self-image.

It is a natural part of childhood that we first form an image of our self. This image typically comes together through our interactions with our parents, brothers and sisters, teachers and other children at times when we are being praised or reprimanded, accepted or rejected, loved or made fun of. As children we have life situations and experiences that we can't understand and we tend to draw wrong conclusions and form a sense of self around these wrong thoughts. "I am not good enough", "Nobody likes me", "I am not pretty enough", "That was stupid of me" or "I am better than you". These wrong thoughts about our self that we agree with stick from childhood and carry into adulthood and as we believe it to be the truth of us, it becomes us. However, our mental image of ourself is not true! The Ego is the false self.

As the Ego takes centre stage in driving our lives, who we really are is simply not seen. We end up living our life through this false idea of our self and it becomes our reality. From this point of view, a massive amount of energy is consumed and a lot of dramas appear in our day-to-day life as we move to protect and enhance who and what we have come to believe our self to be. In this way, the Ego is self-perpetuating.

Hmmm ...

Another way to explain this is that the Ego is a person's sense of self-esteem or self-importance. The Ego is concerned with protecting and enhancing this image of self. It is the part of us that drives us to do things for the purpose of inflating 'who we are' in the eyes of others and ourselves. What is often behind the Ego is fear – the fear of not being accepted or loved by others and perhaps a feeling of lack within ourselves.

The Ego is completely focused on the past or the future and cannot live in the current moment. As a result the Ego thrives in unconsciousness, in our lack of awareness. Ultimately the Ego is that which says no to our experiences, and says no to what is here in this moment as its survival depends upon not investigating the truth of our self – a truth that can only be discovered in the current moment.

Let me boil all this down into one easy statement – ***The Ego is our resistance to What Is.*** [R]

What Is?

Yeah, you know, 'What Is' – The way things are, our circumstances, our situation, our experience in any given moment of time.

The Ego says no to 'What Is'. It is habitually wanting to change the way things are instead of accepting what is here, or putting things off to the future that could be resolved with just a moment of being present right now. *Suffering is born out of our resistance to the way things are.* This is the Ego in action.

The Ego must be running my life!

It's a common situation. But don't be discouraged because the Ego only has power when you are living in the past or focused on the future. With a little awareness your life changes.

I hope so.

Lily, this is why a crisis like cancer can be such a turning point, and a catalyst that changes your life in positive ways. When you face death, you often start to live. The crisis is a demarcation point that is not meant to be the death of you, but the end of those things that keep dramas perpetuating in your life and hold you back from living life to the fullest.

Cancer doesn't seem like such a turning point to me.

I understand your point of view. However, that point of view may change just as mine did, as the Ego becomes humbled and you become more aware.

In my case, the Ego had unknowingly taken over my life, telling me which events were allowed and which were to be denied. The Universe doesn't look at any of life's experiences as good or bad, life experiences are the 'What Is'. In short, *in resisting 'What Is', suffering and disease is born.*[R]

How did you humble the Ego and become aware?

It happened simultaneously, like two ends of a seesaw, with the Ego on one end and awareness on the other. As I became present witnessing things in the moment, awareness grew and the Ego became humbled.

Another way to explain this is that cancer was such an intense crisis point that in the face of death, I stopped resisting and accepted the situation. The Ego is resistance, so as my resistance subsided conscious awareness went up on the seesaw of self. My consciousness shifted as a result.

So we need to face death to humble the ego?

No, absolutely not. The Ego cannot coexist with a state of awareness. The Ego perpetuates in our states of unawareness. It is only when we remain asleep at the wheel that the Ego can hijack our lives. One of the reasons why I am telling you my story is so you can understand the concepts, and then you don't need to go down that path of physical death yourself. The Ego is humbled through conscious awareness, by staying on the watch, observing and exploring your inner thoughts, feelings, sensations and what is happening in your life. This is simply called Consciousness.

OK, how do I get from where I am to consciousness?

It starts with being focused on whatever is here right now, instead of being caught up in the stories from the past or being focused on the future. *Not willing to be with what is here, is the resistance that feeds the Ego, keeps us stuck in the lower rungs of consciousness and perpetuates ill health.*

How do I start? How can I stop focusing on the future when I have cancer?

For me it happened in the shower that day. I didn't have anyone guiding me and I had no knowledge of these things I am sharing with you today. It started when I stopped resisting the situation I was in. I surrendered to 'What is', my life situation and became willing to experience what was here instead of fighting it. This letting go continued in the hospital and Consciousness flowed in. **Consciousness floods in when you let go and become willing to experience whatever is here.**[R]

How can I start?

Well, it's like remembering how to use a muscle you haven't used for a while. For instance, say you were a great tennis player, but now you are fifty years old and you haven't played tennis for twenty years. You think you can't do it anymore because you have forgotten how and you think it's outside your capabilities. How do you re-learn tennis?

You dust off your tennis racket, get down to the tennis court and try it again, play and practice. When you start out, you may hit the ball into the net many times. But slowly those muscles come back and remember how it is done, you gain a bit of strength and confidence, and before you know it, you are playing good tennis once again.

Consciousness is not something you obtain; it is something that's already a part of you, a part that may be hidden like the sun behind the clouds. All you need to do is create a breeze so that the clouds part and there it is.

Awareness is your very nature. It is not something separate from you. There are tools that can help you. If you were just returning to tennis after a long spell, you might buy a new racket and tennis shoes and perhaps you would find someone to guide you, like a good tennis coach. Like a sport you played years ago, connecting with consciousness is something you have already done in the past, so you just need to remember how to do it.

What do you mean I have already done it?

In early childhood you were already in a state of openness, experiencing each moment, connected and aware. But as we grow older and life becomes more complicated and throws up challenges, this awareness gets covered up. So it's just a matter of remembering what we already know. You can use tools like books or the internet to remember, or you could find a good coach, a practitioner who can lead you, or download an app on your phone to guide you. But the best tool of all is free and readily available, and that tool is meditation.

But I have two teenage daughters who need me and a busy career, and now I need to start taking care of my aging mother. My life is already too busy, I have so many responsibilities and I just need to get on with things. I don't have time for meditation, isn't it hard and a lot of work?

No it's the opposite of a lot of work. It's just like riding a bike down a small hill. When you first learn you may get a little frustrated and fall over a few times trying. But soon you find yourself gliding effortlessly without thinking about it. With meditation you move from 'doing' to 'being', and awareness naturally rises as it is entwined with your being, your natural state. We are not called 'Human Beings' by accident.

What can I expect from this meditation and consciousness? What do you experience?

I feel calm, present and connected, like I am plugged into the universe. Have you ever got up early and watched a beautiful sunrise over the ocean with the magnificent florescent orange and yellow reflecting in the clouds over the horizon? That is the kind of infinite peaceful feeling you may sense. A feeling that stays with you even after the sun has passed. When I go surfing, during and after the surf I am in this beautiful space where nothing bothers me. Throughout the day I seem to stay in that state regardless of what other potential disturbing events come along. In this awareness the dramas around me don't stick to me, they just come and go like a cloud in the sky.

Conscious awareness, like 'a witnessing stillness', is hard to describe in words, but once you experience it for yourself, you will get it because consciousness is your very nature.

Ok, I will try.

In surrendering to the situation as I did in the shower and at hospital, I became open and curious to what was happening both inside and outside of me. Little did I know, this was a perfect place to begin.

I found that the shift in consciousness started with my inner experiencing and then was reflected in my outer physical experience.

What do you mean?

My inner feeling of gratitude, the total lack of fear and that inner knowing that I would survive was starting to be reflected in my outer experience in the hospital and in my physical body.

My physical body was undergoing an incredible trauma, one that I was definitely feeling. Around the sixth day in hospital, my physical strength started to return and the colour in my skin became pinker. This miraculous intelligent *healing machine* called my body, started to come back to life.

Most days in hospital, I had visits from family, friends and hospital staff. With each day, I saw the fear in everyone's eyes growing. Near the end of Angelina's daily visit she always asked the same question: "Did you get the results of that lymph node test?" I always responded with a simple unconcerned "No." Finally, on the eighth day she couldn't contain herself any longer and screamed out, "Aren't you concerned?" "Don't you realise how important those tests are!" "This decides our future!" I calmly replied, "Angie, please don't worry, I will be fine. It is hard to explain, but something inside of me is telling me I will be OK. I have never been so sure of something in my life, there is no possibility of being wrong that I will survive".

She looked at me out the side of her eyes and from her expression I think she thought I had lost my mind. But the truth was, I had never been saner in my entire life. The 'insanity' of the controlling Ego was no longer the active driving part of me, for the first time I was seeing and feeling things clearly.

On the morning of my final day in hospital, one of the young interns walked into my room and said: "Steven we are releasing you today, you can pack your things because you are going home!" My intestine had healed to a point where solid food was now passing through it, and my bowel was working again. As a result I could go home.

With that great news, a huge smile lit up my face. As the intern stood in the doorway about to leave, he turned back towards me and said "Oh yeah, I received the results of your lymph node test … and to be honest I am quite surprised, it came back negative, the cancer has not spread!"

With a cheeky confidence I said: "I am not surprised at all, I knew it all along!"

The doctor looked at me curiously, opened his mouth to ask a question, then turned and walked away.

This gratitude and knowing that was part of my inner experiencing was directly reflected in my outer physical experience and my state of health.

So you beat the cancer?

Do you recall what the cells of my body said to me when I was in hospital?

That you will survive?

That I will survive … but … 'to _live_ you must find out what caused the cancer.'

As I left the hospital I didn't understand the importance of the second part of this message " … *to live you must find out what caused the cancer.*" We are not done when we walk out of the hospital door. The true healing comes in treating what caused the situation called cancer.

But you had the operation, wasn't that the end of it?

The operation was about survival, dealing with the emergency of the situation. The doctor dealt with the physical symptoms, which allowed my body to not perish after I had ignored the inner symptoms for over 30 years. Survival is temporary whereas cure is permanent. The operation was not the cure, as what caused my cancer was still an active part of me.

Survival and living are worlds apart. When faced with a life-threatening situation, first we survive the emergency and then move to a cure by uncovering and healing what caused the symptom in the first place. The message from my cells was very clear, that if I did not want to perish, if I was to 'live' I had to find and treat what caused the symptom called cancer. *The key to ensure that your life-threatening situation doesn't reoccur, is to uncover and heal the cause.*

As I walked out of the hospital, those words 'uncover the cause' echoed within, reminding me to remain focused after my time in hospital. To be ready and willing to do whatever it took to ensure I found a cure and never faced cancer again. I had been literally cut wide open, physically 'opened up', in a dramatic event symbolising the digging up and physical remove of all the things I had buried under my thick skin. But what I had buried so deeply was in an energetic form requiring more than just the shovel of the surgeon's knife. So I came to see that the operation was not the end of the line, that *there are two very distinct phases, first survival and then healing the cause.* The real task at hand was just beginning.

~ 9 ~

The sun is always shining behind the clouds

But wasn't your healing a miracle?

It wasn't a miracle in the way that most people think of miracles as being one-off unexplainable supernatural acts. What happened to me is very explainable, and that's why I'm here sharing it with you today. Hopefully you will get some insights that will lead you to discover and heal yourself.

The 'miracle,' the real secret to health, healing and happiness came after I left the hospital. I honestly had no idea what caused the cancer and had no idea where to look. All I knew at this time was that my cells told me I had to find the cause.

So, where did you start, where did you look?

I started by taking time-out. I took some time to just relax and let my physical body heal. I somehow knew that I shouldn't jump back into work and get 'busy' as this was one of my old strategies to avoid things. I felt the need to remain quiet and reflect on what had just happened. What the cells told me about 'uncovering the cause' kept me focused for what was to come.

I had come out of the hospital just happy to be alive, and remained in a state where I was observant and curious. Although I didn't have a plan or know where to start, what I found is that when you live aware in this way, the plan unfolds for you in each moment. So I just relaxed and remained curious about everything that had just happened. Reflection is a process of looking at yourself, and in these days after the hospital, what unfolded was a process of getting to know myself better. Not just the parts of me that I accepted long ago, but also the parts of me that I had resisted and pushed away. Like a child stepping into the forest for the first time, my eyes were wide open willing to discover whatever was there without conditions. Being present with no conditions is a good place to start.

What do you mean 'get to know myself?'

We typically know ourselves in how we interact with the world on this outer physical space. We know and define ourselves by what we have and what we do. We have a wife or a husband, a house, a position with a title. We have kids, a dog, and a car. We go to work, we play sports, we host parties for our friends, and we do things in the physical world. And this is how we typically think of ourselves: in what we do, what we have, and how we interact in the physical world. But there is another part of ourselves that is endlessly vast, and for some reason most of us have never looked, never come to understand the inner often hidden part of ourselves.

When you get to know yourself, what is happening in the outer physical world is no longer a mystery. *Your outer experiences are a reflection of your inner self.*

A common thing I see with people who are experiencing some form of emotional or physical disharmony is that they are willing to do just about anything on the outside to find a solution, but stop at the gates of looking within. With serious illness I see people go through physical operation after operation, take huge amounts of potent drugs as they try to rid themselves of what ails them. All in a rush to get their life back to how it was 'before'. I often wonder why people rush to get life back to the way it was before? 'Before' is where all the conditions existed which led to the threatening situation they are now facing.

Why is this?

People don't want to experience emotional pain. *Our habits and addictions are just a strategy to avoid pain.* What society doesn't teach is that the avoidance of pain is what locks it in and keeps it alive. What I learned from my experience is that **there is nothing wrong with pain, we don't need to avoid it.**[R]

Pain is part and parcel of life. When we open to all of our experiences and are willing to meet whatever the situation brings instead of avoiding it, any hurt is permanently transformed.

Hurt gets transformed to what?

Hurt dissolves. **Become one with the hurt, when you become one with what is here in this moment, hurt, fear, guilt or whatever is**

here, you experience it fully and then it is gone.[R] Avoid the hurt and it stays with you for eternity. Be with the hurt fully and it dissolves.

But I don't want to experience pain or hurt!

Pain is a curious thing. It has us going in all directions outwardly instead of taking a single step inward towards meeting the pain itself. We are most afraid of what we don't know. And since we don't step into this unknown, it remains unknown and we remain afraid to go there. We end up in a kind of Mexican standoff with ourselves. The only winner in this stalemate is the Ego, which is fuelled by our resistance to be with ourselves.

It is the nature of the Ego to be against something, someone or ourselves. What happens when you want to fight cancer and what happens as you resist and avoid your hurts? You feed the Ego, that resistance to life that facilitated the situation in the first place. The real solution is the opposite. It's not being against what is here right now, it's letting go of our resistance to ourselves and those we are against. This is the environment that allows us to become one with 'hurt' and investigate like an innocent child with new eyes. This is the environment that enables permanent healing.

These days when I think of cancer, one of my favourite quotes from a enlightened Indian master named Nisargadatta Maharaj comes to mind. He says: ***"any form of suffering is a call for inner inquiry."*** And this is how we uncover the cause of what troubles us, through curious inquiry and presence.

Why do I feel so reluctant to do this?

Resistance is the reason. The ways we go about avoiding and

numbing our pain has become our habit. And we can be very reluctant to let go of our habits. I too was reluctant, but cancer was confronting enough to get me past this hurdle. It is only our mind that avoids being still and discovering what's here now. The good news is we are not our mind. We are the awareness that observes the mind, so we can let go of resistance through awareness. The mind finds ways to send us in many outward directions, anywhere but being here now with pain because *the mind doesn't understand the vast stillness that is found in the space that exists as we meet anything, including pain.*

I assure you that as you inquire within and meet what is here, past the projections and stories of the mind, you will discover the gems that are inside all of us. Underneath your stories and emotional hurts is the real you that is love, peace and joy.

Really, love, peace and joy?

Lily, I don't want you to believe anything I am sharing with you. Explore and find out for yourself. Then you will know it to be true, not because you heard it but because you have experienced it. To answer your question, Yes. love, joy and a state of peace is what I discovered underneath my emotional hurt after I became present, stopped resisting and investigated.

These things that you are: Love, Joy and Peace, are the very characteristics of higher consciousness. It is the real you being realised past the clouds of lower consciousness that can cover you up.

Our true state is Love. Most people experience profound Love when they look deep into the eyes of a baby. The baby is just being itself without conditioning and when you look into the eyes of a baby you are experiencing the very thing that we are: pure unconditioned Love. Behind the clouds of our mind we are unconditioned Love, beings of joy and peace. Clouds are those things we hold onto through our resistance to them, which hide the sun, our true nature. Regardless of the clouds being there, the sun is always shining brightly behind the clouds. We just need the warm breeze of awareness to blow the clouds away.

So Lily, what I am saying is don't stop at the gates of your inner self. There is nothing to worry about but worry itself. *As you turn inwards you can only find your true self.*[R] The sun will be beaming brightly on the other side of any clouds, and it is the nature of clouds that they appear solid from a distance, but as you approach them you will discover that you move right through them and they dissolve into thin air.

From my own experience of turning inwards, I uncovered that the journey of self-discovery is a beautiful grand adventure.

If our true state is Love, why don't we experience that always?

As a child growing up, there comes a point where we start to wonder who we are. We start to form our own identity, and take on a separate sense of self. In forming our identity, we tend to mimic the gods around us, namely our parents and siblings. We mimic what they do, say and believe. If they are expressing themselves with a life filled with dramas and pain, we take that into our sense of self. If they are expressing themselves with love and happiness, we adopt that too because we are so connected with them, and want to be just like mom and dad. So in forming our identity at a young age, we adopt the ways of our parents. As most parents are not living with a high level of conscious awareness all the time, we take on their unconscious ways. These are the clouds that cover our true state of being.

So it's our parents' fault!

No, this is just human nature. It is not good or bad, it just is. But we do tend to follow our parents ways adopting their beliefs and unconscious habits to form our identity. Once our identity is formed, it becomes solid and we tend to passionately defend the very thing we have come to know ourselves to be. We cling to our beliefs, ideals of how things should and should not be, we cling to 'the stories of me' and play them over and over again supporting the sense of self that we adopted from others. As a result, the clouds of unconsciousness block the sun of the true self within.

It sounds hopeless.

It's not hopeless at all. The clouds can only remain in our resistance. As we unresist and open to what is here, the clouds dissolve. *The universe is intelligent and always striving for balance, it is here ready and willing to bring on the sunshine.* If you cooperate a little bit, the results can be incredible.

Have you ever got a splinter in your toe? It is an interesting thing that if you leave the splinter in your toe, this intelligent healing machine known as your body will push the splinter out all by itself over a period of time. But why not cooperate a little bit? If you have a helpful tool like tweezers, why not help the process along?

The same is true for the emotional hurts that become lodged within us. Like the splinter, this intelligent universe moves to push out our inner hurts.

Really, how does it do that?

The universe is reflective. It is like a big mirror. This universe reflects things to us through our life experiences in order to bring it up to our awareness. It is a big feedback system. With your inner hurts, the universe brings it to your attention to help bring it up and move it out.

How this plays out is that you will experience the same types of emotional hurtful experiences over and over again in your life, until you meet it with awareness. Each repeating experience is the universe reflecting the splinter, bringing it to your attention as an opportunity to heal it. The universe works in such a way that if you become one with the emotional splinter, it is released. In other words, as you meet any hurt with awareness the hurt dissolves.

Is this what happened to you?

Throughout my life, the universe kept bringing me the experience of emotional abandonment through the women in my life. It happened from early childhood, through my teenage years, and into my marriage. It was simply the universe reflecting the invisible splinter that was already lodged inside of me, giving me the opportunity to become aware and heal.

Being aware and observing what's happening in the moment, are the tweezers of consciousness that breaks the cycle of resistance.

But my cancer is physical, it is not an invisible splinter. I have the x-rays to prove it!

You are right Lily, at this point your cancer situation has physical symptoms, but initially those symptoms were invisible and energetic in nature. Over time, as we continue to resist what is behind the invisible splinters, the universe brings us more of the same type of experiences which compound the original splinter. More emotional energetic hurt get poured onto the original splinter which is lodged within our body. Eventually, as we continue to resist, the compounding gets to a point where the invisible energetic entity becomes a visible physical entity that the doctors can detect.

Emotional hurts become cancer?

Have you read any of Eckhart Tolle's books? He uses the term 'Pain Body' to describes what I have been calling 'invisible splinter'. He describes the Pain Body as energetic entities consisting of old emotions, emotional pain, an accumulation of painful experiences that were not fully faced or accepted in the moment it arose. He explains that these energetic entities literally get lodged in our body, in the organs of our bodies.

Yes, emotional hurts can become cancer or some other disease. Disease happens at the crossroads of where you are already hurt and a duration of time. With regards to this, our level of awareness is important. If we remain resistant and unconscious to our emotional hurts, what starts out invisible and energetic in nature can in time become visible and labelled disease.

Does it have to happen this way?

No, of course not. When we live with awareness day-to-day, the hurts are simply faced and accepted in the moment they arise and the emotional energy behind our experiences never get lodged in the organs of the body. The moment we unresist and meet the conflict, permanent healing begins.

It is important to see that all of this is just the universe at play. The universe being reflective in nature, is lovingly showing us what we need to see, so we can cooperate to restore harmony.

Hurts are a part of life, the ebb and flow of the tide. You are not alone, everyone has a past, and everyone has had experiences that shocked and hurt them. These are the things of life, and experiencing is the very reason why we are here. *We are here to experience all aspects of life, and through the experiencing we grow, evolve and rediscover our true nature that shines like the sun.*

~ 10 ~

The responsibility of the finger pointer

So what happened after the hospital?

The first days back at home didn't go well. On my way out of the hospital, I bumped into my doctor and took the opportunity to thank him and give him a big hug. In a passing question I asked what I was allowed to eat when I got home. He replied, "Anything you want".

The next morning my best friend Dave came to visit me and took me on a walk from my house to the ocean front four blocks away. It was a popular beach with a paved promenade that stretched along the beachfront.

I was extremely skinny and had little strength. Before going into hospital I had already lost 20 kilos (44 pounds). Inside the hospital it was 'nil by mouth.' I didn't eat a single thing for nine of the ten days I was there, and as a result I lost another 10 kilos (22 pounds) or so. Mere skin and bones, the muscles in my legs were gone from lack of use, starkly different from my normal athletic body.

As we walked to the promenade, I took tiny baby steps. It was lovely getting the sun on my face again and seeing all the beautiful people walking and exercising.

We ended up sitting on a bench in front of our favourite pub, a place we used to visit once a week. We had our own little spot inside that looked out through a giant glass window we called the fish bowl overlooking the beach, and the constant parade of people coming and going. Dave said jokingly "Maybe a beer will help you heal?" I thought Hmm, I heard that Irish women drink Guinness during pregnancy because of the nutrients, if it's good enough for them, it's good enough for me. After all, the doctor said I could eat whatever I wanted. So we went in and I had two pints of Guinness.

Dave's wife was away that weekend so he showed up at my house later that night with Thai food. We ate green chicken curry and a couple of other medium to hot dishes as we watched the football game on TV. The Thai food tasted amazing after ten days of no food. I ate more than my share.

Later that night at about two in the morning, my stomach let me know it wasn't happy. The combination of Guinness and green chicken curry after ten days of no food was way too much for my system to handle. For the next four days, I became violently ill with vomiting. I couldn't hold any food or water down and ended up losing even more weight from my already skeleton-like frame.

It wasn't a joke then, but now I see the funny side and how asleep at the wheel I still was. Often in the process of becoming conscious, old habits sneak back into our lives, so it's good to remain diligent and aware during this period of waking up to our selves.

But you lost so much weight before the operation because of
Dr. V's wrong diagnosis. I would have been so pissed off! Did
you go after him?

No I didn't. Before the operation I planned on going after him, but
after the operation it was different. I felt a strong sense that going
after Dr V. was not the road I was supposed to take. I was seeing things
differently and had become aligned with a new set of priorities in
life. I started to see my cancer situation as my own responsibility,
not Dr. V's. To get to the cause of cancer, I knew I couldn't point my
fingers at him. I had to rightfully take responsibility.

My Ego was humbled, my perception had changed, and I saw the
facts simply and clearly. The fact is, I had ignored the symptoms for
thirty years and cancer was the result. Cancer didn't appear because
Dr. V. did something to me, cancer came at the end of the line of my
habitual resistance to the hurts that were already there.

A legal battle with Dr. V would have been another form of
resistance that could have easily diverted all of my attention in
an outward direction. If we can be against something, the mind
is enhanced. This is a common escape route from being with
ourselves. *Resistance diverts us from our own inquiry.*

It is important to stay present where we can align with the higher
life-enhancing rungs of consciousness. Because it is at the lower rungs
where disharmony and disease is born in the first place. Aligning with
the positive life-enhancing ways of thinking, speaking and being is
important in healing any form of disharmony. As you move forward
in life with consciousness, one day you will look back at the way things
were, and scratch your head wondering why you put some much of
your time and energy into avoiding life the way it was.

Soon after my green chicken curry experience, I phoned my friend Hinka, a Dutch lady who owned an I.T. contracting company that I worked with on many of my software development projects. We had become close friends and I told her I had just returned from hospital where I had had an operation for bowel cancer. This caught her by surprise and she replied, "Right, I will be right over."

Hinka arrived on my doorstep with a duffle bag full of books. The bag was so big and heavy she had to drag it up the steps into my house. And the books were not just any books, these were books about life, spirituality, natural health and healing, meditation, cancer, nutrition and much more. She walked into the door, gave me a heartfelt hug and she said "You will have a lot of time in bed in the coming month, plenty of time to read some of these books. I will come back in a couple of weeks to see how you are."

So, each day over the next few weeks, I reached into this bag and picked out a book at random. The first couple were about cancer and people's personal stories. When I started reading these, I knew that 'cancer' itself was not my issue, and reading people's accounts of their cancer didn't interest me.

I read a few books about nutrition, juicing and the like. This was important after the Guinness and curry disaster, and from these books I started to enhance my diet.

I read some books about the power of the mind and various spiritual subjects, which were all completely new to me. And then I picked up a book about meditation. I read the first couple of chapters and found it interesting. Something inside of me was drawn to the concept of meditation, but as I had never experienced it, I had trouble comprehending the words in the book. After a couple chapters, I put the book back into the bag with the idea of exploring meditation sometime in the future.

True to her word, Hinka showed up at my doorstep two weeks later. She came inside and over a cup of tea we talked about my state of health, the operation and my plans going forward. The fact was I didn't have a plan, I was just sitting around watching TV, letting the physical wounds heal so I could return to work.

Hinka had other ideas. She said I should get away, take some space for a couple of weeks to rest and reflect on what had just happened. She told me this would be very healing. She said her twin sister named Ninka lived in Byron Bay, and suggested that I go up and stay with her for a while.

I told Hinka that I couldn't go away for two weeks, and that I had a family I was responsible for. And besides this, I was sure Angelina wouldn't let me go.

Hinka calmly said "Why don't you ask her tonight and see what she says?"

So that night, as Angelina was making dinner, I walked into the kitchen and told her about Hinka's proposition.

Without skipping a beat, Angelina replied, "Do it!"

I was stunned.

~ *11* ~

Destiny through the doorway of the heart

I flew a few days later, taking a propeller plane to the country town of Ballina located about twenty kilometres south of Byron Bay. I couldn't believe my eyes as I walked into this tiny one room country airport. Hinka was waiting there to greet me. I scratched my head wondering how the hell she got here because she had dropped me off at the airport in Sydney. We greeted each other with a big hug. As we let go of each other, she looked me in the eyes and said enthusiastically, "Hi I'm Ninka, Hinka's sister, nice to meet you".

Hinka and Ninka — really?

True. Life is stranger than fiction. I couldn't make this up. They weren't just twins, they were completely identical in every way. As we drove to Byron Bay along the ocean coast road, Ninka told me about the area and how it is known for being a mixed community of old hippies, surfers, backpackers and natural health practitioners.

I couldn't help but notice the way she spoke, the way she held her head, the look in her eye, and all the little mannerisms and nuances were exactly the same as Hinka's. It was freaky but strangely comforting. Ninka was so much like Hinka, she felt like an old friend from the moment we met. Those twins took me under their wings, two angels sent to guide me.

Ninka helped me to regain my energy and then introduced me to two of the most important people who changed the course of my life. One of those was Dr. Rahasya Fritjof Kraft who lived in the Byron Bay area.

We arrived at Ninka's humble two-bedroom house located a few blocks back from the beach. Her small back yard had been converted to a thriving organic garden bursting with life. She walked me through it, collecting fruit and vegetables. To help restore my energy and health, Ninka introduced me to live foods and raw vegetable juicing. This really worked wonders for me.

In her back yard she had trays and trays of something that looked like grass which she called wheatgrass, the main ingredient in her daily juice. She took her scissors and cut some of the wheat grass as if she was cutting someone's hair. As we headed back into her house, she plucked a lemon off the tree and put it in the tray I was carrying which was already overflowing with fresh carrots, beetroot, celery, capsicum and garlic.

She made the juice using a juicing machine. The colour of the juice was a dark green brown. I took one look at it and was completely turned off. But I was her guest and open to try new things, so I gave it a go.

I took my first sip and it was awful. The wheatgrass was really overpowering, but she tried to soften it by adding a bit more fruit, carrots and lemon and I managed to get it down.

Ninka told me that she juices twice a day and that it is a great way to detox the body of chemicals and restore the minerals and nutrients we need. She said the body holds onto things within the organs and when you feed the body 'live' raw foods, it kicks the body into gear so that it cleanses itself by releasing the toxins.

Around dinner she made another juice with a slightly different recipe. Surprisingly, a couple of sips into it, I found that I didn't mind the taste at all.

The next couple of days, I just hung around Ninka's house, taking walks on the beach and swimming in the ocean a couple of times a day. At times I became suddenly tired and would lie down and sleep. I had no agenda, no timetable, and no responsibilities. It was a great break, just what I needed to help recover from the trauma of the operation.

At Ninka's, I started listening to what my body was telling me, reading books and taking naps throughout the day and just hanging out talking with Ninka. Like her sister, Ninka also had a private collection of books in the same genres of healing, spirituality and natural health. And they both had a huge passion for helping others.

I was getting into the juicing routine. We had juice at breakfast, lunch and a bit more around sunset. On the third day of this routine, a substance with the constitution of sand started coming out of me when I had a bowel movement. It was like tiny granular bits of sand and it continued to come out of me for the next three days.

At the end of the week I told Ninka about this. She was not surprised and told me that it was good news; my body was releasing toxins that she suspected were from the pancreas or the kidneys.

The funny thing was, within about a week of being with Ninka on this juicing routine, I felt my energy return and stabilise. I was getting stronger and feeling better every day and I had lots of quiet time to reflect on everything that had happened. It was the first time in my life that I can recall where I allowed myself to stop, relax, reflect and just be. In a strange way, cancer was the excuse I needed to allow myself to stop running.

How interesting. And what about those two people who changed your life?

Yes, there were two special people Ninka introduced me to who I feel I was destined to meet.

Destined?

Yes, like a hand from the universe coming down to help me, making sure certain events took place. *As you cooperate with life, life cooperates with you.*

After the first week with Ninka my energy had returned. The next morning I woke up and Ninka said "Steven, I have a few things planned for us today. I have booked you into a meeting with Bryant Hopley who is the local Naturopath. You can talk to him about food and nutrition and learn about what is best for you to eat. After that, I will take you to Mullumbimby to meet a man named Dr. Rahasya Kraft, known around Byron Bay as Rahasya. The word on the street of Byron Bay from people in the know is that Rahasya is the most enlightened person in the region.

I just shrugged my shoulders and said, "OK" and didn't think much of it.

Bryant Hopley was a small-framed man in his forties. His eyes looked intelligent and kind, and he reminded me of a wise owl.

Bryant didn't know anything about me, or my condition, so he asked me a few questions and then started to examine me. Bryant was also an Iridologist, which is the science that uses the eyes to identify the status of the body, health and conditions. He used a special microscope to look at the patterns, colours and characteristics of the iris, from this he learned about my state of health and current condition.

After looking at my eyes for a while, he said, "You have a very strong constitution. Your body is well put together, except I see one place that is weak. There is a kink in the Sigmoid colon which represents the large intestine in the pelvic area". The patterns within my eyes told Bryant the story of cancer, which was located in the Sigmoid colon.

I was keen to learn about nutrition, what I should eat and what I should avoid to help me recover fully and achieve maximum ongoing health. He talked about nutrition and specific foods for the first half of the meeting, I diligently wrote down his every word. He had a wealth of knowledge and shared it willingly.

Unexpectedly our discussion changed focus and he started talking about human emotions, our emotional state and how important our closest relationships are. He started drawing a picture on a white board explaining the importance of relationships, specifically the importance of communication and intimacy within relationships and their effect on health.

He said: ***"Cancer is a tap on the shoulder both physically and emotionally."*** The factors to consider on the physical side were: dietary, deficiencies in modern food, fitness, chemicals in life, smoking and drinking. He said that emotions were most important to health and healing. The factors on the emotional side that I needed to look at were: Is my life in good shape? Are there any suppressed emotions? Are my relationships healthy? Is the communication within those relationships healthy? Is my spiritual side healthy?

Bryant spent most of our remaining time together ensuring I understood the direct relationship between emotions and the physical body. He explained how the emotions have a direct biochemical effect on the physical. He was the first to share with me that disease in the physical body is often a direct reflection and result of internal emotional issues. He reflected upon why I experienced bowel cancer, explaining that the bowel is the place where our emotions are often stored.

Bryant then drew me a picture representing what he was sharing. He drew what he called the three pillars to health: emotions, diet and fitness. Between these three pillars lies a balance between work, rest and play. All of this sits within Spirituality, our essence, the deepest values and meaning by which we live.

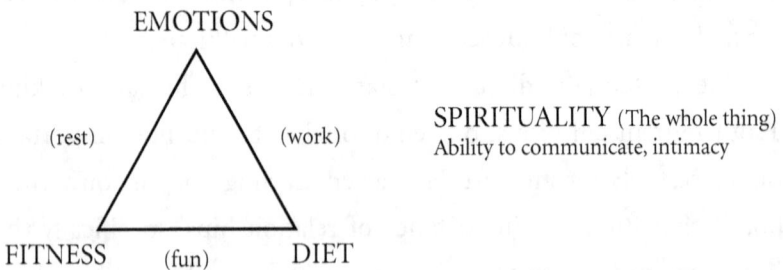

EMOTIONS

(rest)   (work)   SPIRITUALITY (The whole thing)
                                Ability to communicate, intimacy

FITNESS   (fun)   DIET

He then introduced the word consciousness to me. He explained that we can expand our consciousness to the extent that we control our own destiny. He talked about meditation and how it was a way to integrate these things in the triangle.

I was spellbound and amazed that he cared so much for me that he shared this deeper wisdom. How eye opening that he talked about emotions, relationships, communication and love and their importance to health. I knew that he was speaking the truth, because when you hear truth you know it.

The meeting was scheduled for one hour, but I had been with him for two and a half hours. The receptionist knocked on the door and told Bryant that she couldn't postpone the other patients any longer. As I got up from my chair to leave, I looked into his eyes and thanked him from my heart. He returned my gaze and said "Steven, it is so refreshing to meet someone who really wants to heal, thank you".

What did he mean by 'someone who really wants to heal'?

I didn't know at the time, as I assumed everyone who was unwell simply wants to heal. But the human mind is very interesting, and what I found out years later is that people often quietly take on the identity of their illness which gives them a new sense of self.

Why?

Unconsciously, they gain something from taking on the identity of their illness. People come to know them as their ongoing illness and illness story. In adding this to their identity, people receive attention, special treatment and certain things that they may feel they are lacking, like a feeling of being loved and accepted by others for example. Once this happens it's a tricky situation because outwardly they may say they want the illness to end, but subconsciously they may not want the illness to end because that would annihilate the very thing they have come to know themselves to be.

Our attachment to our sense of self, the identities we take on to define our self, is our biggest addiction, and we will fight tooth and nail to hold onto the 'self' we believe we are. A common result is that we end up holding onto the illness that now defines us. This is a big reason why people resist becoming present and looking inwards, because to see the truth would end the self they have become.

Beyond the thoughts about our self that we agree with, lies the unknown. Letting go of the identities we have become comfortable with means stepping into unknown territory, and for most people it is a scary proposition to not know 'Who Am I'. In other words, the ending of the illness that has become a part of who they are would be a kind of death of them.

So what Bryant Hopley was saying in a roundabout way is that I had not become 'cancer', I was not attached to this label, nor did I define myself by it like a proud wounded warrior. I saw cancer for what it was, a situation that had come into my life at this moment in time. Having already faced and accepted death, I surely wanted to heal and live.

Interesting. And the second person, when did you meet Dr. Kraft?

We went to see Dr. Rahasya Kraft right from Bryant Hopley's office. I walked out the front door and Ninka was waiting for me. She was a little stressed because we were already late for our meeting with him. She drove very fast out of Byron Bay to the place we were meeting him.

On the way, she told me more about Rahasya. He was a highly

acclaimed medical doctor from Germany. Ninka being a Byron Bay local for over ten years, was on the inside track to the best healers in the area. She told me that the whispers on the street by those in the know, was that Rahasya was the real deal, an enlightened master.

Enlightened?

Ninka didn't go into too much explanation about what this meant, she simply said that he was aware at a high level, that he had access to insights and higher wisdom that flows through him effortlessly at that level of consciousness he had realised. In other words, he was a self-realised person, who can point you directly to the truth.

What do you mean self-realised?

Lets just say that there are no clouds that stick around Rahasya's being. As a result, he lives in a state of pure awareness, a state where you realise a high form of yourself associated with the highest rungs of consciousness. At such levels of consciousness, his perception is heightened giving him access to universal wisdom and intelligence.

At the time I didn't really care that he was enlightened. Although it sounded impressive, I didn't understand what it meant, but soon after I met him I found out.

About ten minutes out of town, Ninka drove up a steep, windy, dirt road with lots of pot holes. A forest of trees lined the road and a few minutes later we pulled up to a magnificent spot on top of a hill in front of a beautiful wooden building called *Mevlana*.

We were quite late and nobody seemed to be around, so I got out and peaked through a large window into a big open room with a couch in the centre against the wall, some sound equipment, microphones and more. There were a number of chairs scattered about the place, but nobody was inside.

Mevlana is a beautiful property. There were sweeping views of the forest-filled valley and in the distance some mountains and an extinct volcano. In the past, volcanic eruptions had deposited a rich mix of ash and crystal sediment across the region. Everything at Mevlana was thriving, the trees seemed larger, the grass was greener, tropical plants thrived and wild flowers flourished in this magnificent spot.

As I was standing there taking it all in, a man dressed in white came from around the corner into the courtyard and approached me.

I had never met an enlightened person before, so I didn't know what to expect. Rahasya walked up to me and smiled and said "Hi, I am Rahasya, are you Steven?"

After a handshake we walked around the side of the building and stepped into a small room for us to have a consultation.

Besides being a successful medical doctor in Germany, Rahasya was a famous therapist and spiritual teacher amongst other things across Asia and Europe. The hinterland of Byron Bay was his home and a place where he mainly rested for a few months each year when he wasn't travelling the world teaching and healing. So I was lucky he was in town and agreed to meet with me.

He was wearing loose fitting white pants and a matching top. He looked clean-cut, with no facial hair or anything that stood out as weird. He was about my height, six foot tall, thin, fit and healthy from what I could see. He seemed like a normal guy in most aspects except there was something about him that I picked up on instantly; there was a kind of eminence that came from him. It wasn't anything that said "Look at me, I am special," it was more subtle, real and a kind of positive energy that was a part of him. I sensed a feeling of peace around him and I could see that he had nothing to prove. To summarise it now, he is someone who is simply living truth, in a total state of awareness.

We walked into the consultation room. The inside walls and entry door were covered by white drapes and two chairs stood facing each other.

Rahasya asked me to take a seat. I felt a little apprehensive. I had never done anything like this before and I didn't know what to expect. Yet at the same time I was curious and decided to stay open. I hadn't forgotten what the cells of my body told me. I truly wanted to find the cause of the cancer to cure it, and was willing to explore new things.

After some initial introductions, Rahasya looked me in the eyes and said, "Well Steven, why are you here?"

I told him that I have read a little about meditation and find it curious and want to learn more about it.

He asked me what I thought meditation was.

I told him I was not really sure. That I heard meditation is something that helps you relax and reduces stress. I told him that I read about it in a book but found it difficult to understand. I asked if he could explain it to me.

He said that meditation is our natural state, where we allow everything to be as it is. In allowing everything to be as it is, you allow the body to be as it is, whatever it feels, whatever the sensations are, you allow them. You allow your feelings to be what they are, and allow all the thoughts to be what they are. You allow everything to be as it is.

He shared that we all know how to allow everything to be as it is because we do it each night when we go to bed. As we fall asleep each night we just let go and allow everything to be as it is. Meditation is much the same, we just let go, however instead of falling asleep, we discover the wakefulness within this relaxed state of allowing everything as it is.

He shared that this wakeful relaxed allowing enables us to experience things that we normally keep at bay in our day-to-day resistance to 'everything as it is'. So in meditation we just let go, we let things be, and a mysterious door opens to who we have always been.

I have tried meditation and I just can't do it, I can't stop my mind from having thoughts.

That is a common misunderstanding about meditation. In more recent years, Rahasya has taught me that there are meditation techniques where you focus on the breath, or where you try to still your mind and try rid your mind of thoughts. He says that this is not the point because meditation is not about achieving anything, it is not about doing, it is about being. It is an excuse to allow everything to be as it is. You can't 'do' meditation, because doing is a becoming and a product of the mind. You just sit silently, usually with your eyes closed and witness whatever is here. No goal, no need to change whatever is happening in your feelings, sensations or thoughts, you just witness and allow everything to be as it is.

Rahasya used an analogy to explain meditation in a way that I really connected with. Rahasya and I are both surfers and he said that meditation is like surfing a wave. As you catch a wave you become completely present in the moment with the wave and the active thinking mind naturally goes to the background. You become one with the wave and experience a moment of no time, kind of like an interval or space between the seconds of time. He said that surfing is a type of meditation, and this is why people get so hooked on surfing, because of the peace and vastness they experience in being one with the moment, one with nature, experiencing their true nature that exists as we allow everything to be as it is.

I shared my understanding of what he was saying through my own experience of surfing. While in the surf sitting on my board half submerged in the ocean, I merge with nature. While riding a wave, I am fully in that moment not thinking, just interacting with the wave in that moment. I shared that after surfing, when I get out of the surf, nothing bothers me all day long. No matter what happens, I remain peaceful, calm, energised and feel connected.

Then the conversation switched gears. Rahasya asked me a very potent question: "So Steven you recently had cancer ... Tell me, if you had died, what is it that you would have missed the most?"

What a question!

Yes, this question went straight to my heart. I had never thought about it before. Without blinking the answer was right there, "My kids. It is my kids that I would miss the most."

He asked, "What is it about your kids that you would miss the most?"

I explained that I have a connection with them that is so special, a connection unlike anything else I have experienced in my life. It is a heightened connection, literally out of this world!

He dug a little deeper by asking me "what is this connection, can you describe it?"

I looked away briefly and then answered: "Yes … it's Love!"

He guided me even deeper asking me "what's so unique about this Love that it is so special and unlike anything else you have experienced? What is this thing you describe as 'out of this world'?"

I closed my eyes for a bit, and it came clearly to me what it was. "It's unconditional. Unconditional Love."

Rahasya said "Very good, lets use this feeling of Unconditional Love and try a little experiment in meditation. Close your eyes and take some deep breaths."

We paused in silence for a while. Then he asked me, "where in your body do you feel this Unconditional Love?"

I placed my hand over my heart.

"Describe what it feels like, what are the sensations in the body, and what are you seeing or experiencing in the moment?"

I described to him what I was feeling and seeing. I recall that there was this beautiful encompassing warmth emanating from my heart area. I saw movement and colours behind my eyes. They weren't any particular objects that were familiar, they were more like streams of clouds of various shapes that were floating around. The objects themselves were not solid, but transparent and had no real meaning to me. The shapes were moving in different directions with similar properties of soft fluffy smoke in different shapes, coming in and fading out, floating around, but no fixed physical form that you could reach out, touch or describe as something I was familiar with.

Rahasya asked me to take a picture of what I was seeing, and to put the picture in a frame and then hang it on a door that was in front of me. He then asked me to reach out, open the door and walk through it.

Within the meditation, I took that image and then hung it as a picture on the door in front of me and walked through the door. In this new room the view changed. The colours were different, the image was altered and I described it to him.

After my description of the place I was now experiencing, Rahasya guided me deeper. He said there was a curtain in front of me and to reach out and step through the curtain. As I did this, I entered yet another place, another room within me. And again it was different from the other rooms. Being guided by Rahasya, I walked through room after room describing what I was seeing, feeling or experiencing.

In the meditation I had no concept of time, but to guess I would say after 30 minutes or so I stepped through a door into a room of nothingness. It was infinitely vast, endless and dark. Rahasya asked me what I was seeing and feeling. I waited and waited for something to show up. Finally I said to him "Nothing. I don't see anything, just an incredible endless vastness".

Rahasya said softly: "You are there."

In that moment, I let go, and an incredible thing happened. Suddenly I could see everything even though my eyes were closed. It was as if I was in the room but outside of my body. I could see myself in the room sitting in front of Rahasya. There was an orange light surrounding my body and I saw myself sitting in the chair encircled by orange light. It was translucent, some sort of energy and was moving and alive. It was spinning around me in a circular motion.

What did it feel like?

I felt incredible. It was the most beautiful thing I have ever experienced to this day. The best word I can find to describe it is bliss, complete and utter bliss. I was it, me at my deepest level of being, touched in meditation. As I sat still in meditation with my eyes closed observing this, I couldn't stop smiling. So blissful, I could have happily stayed in that state forever. The energy continued to spin around me, like a cocoon of unconditional love. After some time, Rahasya spoke to me softly and slowly guided me out of the meditation, back to physical reality.

As I opened my eyes, we just sat there in silence looking at each other, each of us with big smiles on our faces. That meditation allowed me to experience a part of me I had forgotten, yet had known before.

As the session came to a close, Rahasya said he felt something, some issue that had to do with my wife. He invited me to come back the next day to explore it. I accepted immediately and without resistance.

~ 12 ~

The Guru,
Dr. Rahasya Fritjof Kraft

Is Rahasya some kind of Guru?

He is a classically trained German medical doctor, a famous therapist, an expert on the mind and it's workings, and a highly sought after enlightened teacher running courses all around the world helping people discover and heal themselves. He has a deep understanding regarding the ways of the universe and our interplay with it, so he brings quite a broad understanding and perspective when it comes to life, the human condition, health and healing.

Soon after meeting him, I too became very curious about Rahasya. That very night after my first meditation with him, I was back at Ninka's house and she invited her friend Kate over for dinner. Kate happened to be a long time friend of Rahasya, and had met him many years ago in India where they were both living, studying and exploring themselves through spirituality. Kate said that Rahasya was the name given to him by an enlightened Indian master.

She shared that Rahasya had worked as a conventional medical doctor for many years in Germany, first in a leading hospital and then three years in his own general practice. While in his general practice, Rahasya was offered a five-year contract as the head of the intensive care unit in one of the most prestigious hospitals in Germany at the base of the Alps. Friends and envious colleagues congratulated him for being offered 'the best job in Germany,' but something inside Rahasya felt conflicted and he realised he had to reject this offer. He had become somewhat disillusioned with the approach of conventional medicine. What he experienced at the highest level of the profession was that mainstream medicine focuses on the 'after effects' of ill health and not the cause of people's health issues. To him this approach completely missed the point and was not why he had decided to become a doctor.

Rahasya chose to become a doctor to heal people. He didn't become a doctor just to treat symptoms or to be a highly paid prescription pusher. His interests lay in curing the cause of people's ill health. He knew that in dealing with the cause, you wouldn't have to treat the after effects, the physical manifestation called disease.

So at the peak of his medical career, he walked away. Germany is a very structured society, so of course everyone thought he had gone mad. But to his credit, he followed his heart. He not only turned down this prestigious position he was offered, he left behind a very successful medical practice and began to travel, searching for the answers, with a focus on uncovering the causes of man's ill health.

Did he find it?

Yes, I am a good example of this. Much of what I am sharing with you today Rahasya taught me or pointed me towards, and I then explored and experienced myself. As you will soon see, my advanced cancer was cured as a result of Rahasya's guidance.

Rahasya's search for answers eventually took him to India where he became a student in an ashram, a small community focused on study, healing, self exploration, yoga, music and other spiritual pursuits under the direct guidance and teachings of an enlightened master. Rahasya lived and learned there for ten years. During this time his state of consciousness shifted to a very high level, bringing to him a broader perspective and higher wisdom aligned with a greater understanding of the human condition, and a deep understanding of the workings and causes of man's disharmony and ill health.

Rahasya soon became part of the core circle of people that were responsible for creating and teaching the most important advanced courses within the Ashram's school. Amongst other things, Rahasya became a famous therapist, teacher and a practicing doctor working both inside and outside of the Ashram in India.

After ten years of learning, teachings and healing, he knew it was time to bring this understanding to the world. With his sharp intellect, vast experience and bag of tools from his medical background coupled with conscious understanding of how to heal the real causes of man's suffering, he left India and started to teach others across the globe, showing people how to cure the cause of their inner and outer disharmony forever.

He has been running courses across the world ever since. Healing and enabling people to awaken to their truth. During these travels he came to Australia and discovered Byron Bay where he settled with his wife Nura in the vicinity of Wollumbin, the central core of the largest ancient extinct volcano in the southern hemisphere, which is commonly known today as Mount Warning. Wollumbin is an Aboriginal word meaning 'Cloud Catcher', an appropriate place for Rahasya to live and teach as *all that separates us from our truth and health are the clouds within our inner sky.*

~ 13 ~

The invitation

So did you go back to see Rahasya the next day?

I went back to Mevlana for the follow up session, but this time as I entered the room I noticed three seats. Two chairs were facing each other, and a large cushion faced the two chairs.

He asked me to sit down on the cushion facing the two chairs as he sat in another chair off to the side.

In our session the previous day, he felt something when I talked about my wife and he suggested we explore this by using a technique called Voice Dialogue. Voice dialogue is a way to become aware and embrace the various parts of our selves that we normally are not aware of. And through dialogue, I was able to explore the situation with my wife.

Your wife was there?

No, she was at home in Sydney about eight hours away.

Rahasya held a brief meditation to create the space for the

session. He said that one of the two empty chairs represented me and the other chair represented Angelina. He didn't say which was which, that was something I would decide, and surprisingly I knew instantly that the chair to my left was me, and the chair to the right was Angelina.

How did you know?

It wasn't my mind telling me this, it was a strong feeling that my chair was on the left, and her chair was on the right.

I was invited to choose and sit in one of the two chairs. On his invitation, I chose to sit in the chair to the left, the chair that represented me. As I sat down in that chair I felt all of my feelings, all of my stories in relation to Angelina. I felt enraged, forceful, betrayed, hurt and a number of other things. The issue of the cancer came right to the surface and Rahasya asked me to speak to Angelina as if she was sitting in front of me in the other chair. He asked me to tell her what I was feeling inside. While I faced Angelina's chair, I spoke to her about how hurt and betrayed I felt. I got quite angry as I spoke to her and said things to her that I had been holding in for a long time.

As I finished speaking, Rahasya invited me to take the other chair, to sit in the chair representing Angelina. As I sat in that chair a transformation occurred. I could feel Angelina's feelings. I felt meek and scared in regard to what Steven had just said. Rahasya asked Angelina to share what she was feeling and experiencing. But sitting in Angelina's chair, the words couldn't come out because crying took over. All of the stuff around the cancer and what happened in America was too overwhelming. From her perspective there was no betrayal, she was put into a threatening situation and was just trying to cope with it.

As the session ended, I had a new perspective into the situation at hand. Most important were the insights obtained from Angelina's point of view. I had been quietly pointing the finger at Angelina as the cause of my cancer, and from a new perspective this interpretation started to shift a little.

As we stepped outside the door of the session room, Rahasya handed me a one page leaflet, at the top it read: 'Counselling for Counsellors course – Counselling from the Heart'. As I glanced at the leaflet and looked up at Rahasya he said, "Steven, this Sunday I am starting a six day course called 'Counselling from the Heart,' I invite you to attend".

I looked down at the leaflet again and read more of the detail about the course. It was a counselling training course for professional counsellors, social workers, doctors, nurses and practitioners. This course brought together many of the most important teachings Rahasya learned in his years as a Medical Doctor, Therapist and his time as a practitioner and teacher in India. It combined practical counselling techniques utilising advanced meditation, synchronicity, connecting at the heart, communication facilitation skills and a whole bunch of other things. After reading the leaflet I wondered why he invited me of all people. I didn't feel ready for such an advanced course. I questioned him "This course is geared toward professional counsellors, doctors and nurses and utilises advanced meditation, I have only meditated twice, why have you invited me to come to this?"

Rahasya said, "Steven, I wouldn't have invited you if you were not ready. But make no decision right now, go home and meditate on it and the answer will come."

~ 14 ~

The mind is in service
to the heart

Did you take the course?

On the way home from that meeting with Rahasya, I said to myself there was no way I'm going to take that course!

Why not?

It was way outside of my comfort zone. I wasn't ready for such a thing, or at least that's what I thought.

Subconsciously I was resisting the whole idea of really facing what was behind my cancer. After all I had been running away from it for 30 years. So in that moment, I told myself a story that I wasn't ready and didn't have the required skills for such a course. *The Ego behind our resistance is very creative in keeping us away from being still and finding peace.*

After returning to Ninka's house, it started raining and we had a two-day heavy tropical downpour. Too wet to go outside, I stayed mostly in my bedroom reading books, sleeping and writing my thoughts in a journal.

It was still a few days before Rahasya's counselling course began and I had been thinking about Rahasya's invitation. The more I thought about it, the more uncomfortable I became with the whole idea. After analysing the leaflet for the tenth time, my mind said "NO WAY!" and I decided to pass on his offer.

Later that afternoon with it still raining hard outside and with nothing much else to do I decided to experiment with meditation. It was my first meditation without Rahasya guiding me. I sat on my bed in an upright position and put my hands on my lap. I closed my eyes and took a couple of long, deep, slow breaths. After a while everything went quiet and then suddenly it appeared: a vivid picture with a message.

A framed picture appeared within me. The picture was of a tree lined country road in a thick wooded area. The road started at the bottom left side of the picture frame and travelled straight up through the middle of the picture cutting a path through the forest of trees and bush. About three-quarters to the top of the picture, the road veered to the right and ended at the very top right corner of the frame. The strange thing was the road was so densely tree-lined that the top branches of the trees reached across the road forming a canopy, a tunnel of trees approximately 6 metres (20 feet) above the road.

The canopy was so thick it blocked out most of the sun, giving the road a very dark, cold and eerie feeling. Further ahead where the road veered off to the right, the canopy of trees became thinner, and towards the top right of the picture the canopy vanished, and the road was full of light, sunny and welcoming.

My heart skipped a beat as I knew what the picture meant ... Rahasya's course ... the light at the end of the tunnel! Although it was dark and scary right now where I stood, it was the road I had to take, the light was at the end of the tunnel.

The picture was etched in my mind as I came out of the meditation. I knew what to do. The rational part of me was still screaming, 'No!' Yet a deeper part of me was saying, 'Yes!' For once I had to ignore logic, and trust a part of me I was just coming to know: my heart. I accepted the invitation and booked into the course.

~ 15 ~

Peeling the onion brings happy tears

What part of you was screaming No?

My egoic mind, the very thing within me that had been resisting life for so long was once again resisting. The mind and its endless analysis, stories, past/future orientation and fear of the unknown, screamed No because rationally this course was outside the comfort zone that it knew about, felt comfortable with and could control.

Meditation allows you to step past the mind's constrictions. In meditation, we are simply present with whatever is here right now. *It is when we go past the active thinking mind, allowing everything to be as it is, that we enter the unknown place, where our truth is revealed.*

At Ninka's house this is what happened. I became still, went into meditation and allowed everything to be as it is. In connecting to consciousness in this way, the path for me appeared in a picture with a bright light at the end of the tunnel. I couldn't ignore that clear message. From that space there was no fear or resistance, and I signed up to the course.

Ninka decided to take the course too. Two days later we arrived together for the Counselling from the Heart Course.

The course was held at Mevlana?

Yes. When we arrived on the first day people were milling around in the front courtyard just in front of the main room where the course was to be held. Stepping inside Mevlana Hall, it was warm and inviting, the architecture was beautiful, cathedral ceilings, polished cherry wooden floors, grand windows allowing the sunlight to enter and fill the room, fresh flowers and a couple of beautiful statues of Buddha completed the room. People were quiet, sipping cups of tea and generally keeping to themselves as we waited for the course to begin.

In the centre of the room against the wall was a two-seater couch. On the floor in front of the couch was a large Indian rug. On top of that was a coffee table with flowers, candles and a large microphone. On each side of the couch were speakers connected to a professional stereo system.

In front of the couch were rows of those 'L' shaped chairs with no legs. Of the 30 students attending, many brought their own cushions to sit on.

Rahasya came in and sat down on the right hand side of the couch. He had an assistant with him who sat to his left. Her name was Karima and she was fascinating to look at. She reminded me of a wise American Indian. She had a naturally tanned skin with deep green eyes and thick streaky black hair that went down to her waist. She was tall and fit and had a real presence about her.

We took our seats on the floor in front of Rahasya and Karima. There were students from all walks of life. Many were practising professionals in the fields of counselling, psychology, medicine, social welfare and the like. A third of the students were not medical or professional counsellors, they were a mix of locals that included business people, housewives, spiritual seekers, hippies and other people who were searching for answers or on the path to becoming a counsellor. Looking around the room, I felt like the greenest of the bunch; all of this was new to me. I walked into this course with a blissful naivety without any expectations. *No expectations is a great vantage point for any exploration.*

Rahasya started the day by guiding us into a meditation to create the space for what would unfold. When there are thirty people meditating in a magical setting like Mevlana, it is very easy to let go and let things flow.

Most days followed a similar pattern. We started with a meditation, and then Rahasya would begin the day's lessons, teaching us the art of counselling from the heart. He brought a lot of practical knowledge integrated with incredible wisdom and an array of different techniques and tools that allow the counsellor and the client to form a heart connection, thus enabling the client to relax, let go, and step into the unknown to uncover the hidden treasures of meeting what is here. Much of what we learned was very simple and natural, and I guess that is part of the beauty and power of Rahasya's teachings, it's like nature itself.

Rahasya taught us how to use meditation as a tool to start each consultation. This was an important part of each counselling session because it did two things, it created the space where truth and understanding can unfold, and it allowed both the counsellor and client to get past their active thinking rational mind, to connect at the heart level and be with what is here. All this allows things to unfold where the client taps into an awareness that is often masked out by rationality.

During the course I remember Rahasya teaching us about running a counselling session and the importance of creating the space and connecting with the client at the heart level. He taught us about 'Synchronicity of the Heart', which is the space of unconditional love, an impersonal space of love created between the counsellor and the client where the healing happens.

To create this environment for healing, the counsellor goes into his heart deeper than all the stories where he naturally meets a vast and peaceful emptiness. In this emptiness he merges with the emptiness in the client's heart. Rahasya calls it the empty heart, the true self that is aware of all experience and naturally welcomes everything as it is. Within this space of love, healing naturally unfolds.

So the counsellor opens his heart with compassion and unconditional love to the client connecting energetically in the heart space. The counsellor is there to mainly listen with a compassionate heart. And if the client gets lost during their self-discovery, the counsellor is there to gently lead them back. Interestingly, the counsellor does not 'solve' the client's issues, that happens naturally for the client on its own in this space of presence and Love.

How does it happen naturally on its own?

It is the nature of Consciousness. When you become still, when you are here now with What Is, without a goal, without wanting to change whatever is found, then what we have been harbouring inside no longer needs to be hidden. In a way we bring a light to it and see it for what it is. Our inner conflicts simply resolve in this way. You could say that *consciousness is like a light that dissolves what is hidden in the dark inside.*

For two to three hours each morning, Rahasya taught us this art of counselling which combined everything he learned and had been successfully applying around the world. Daily he introduced new techniques and new wisdom, and then we put the theory into practice through live exercises where we participated in real counselling sessions. In these exercises students took turns alternating between being the counsellor running the session and being the client having the counselling session. Just learning on a theoretical level is not really learning, the teachings need to be put into practice for it to become experienced and understood. *Once experienced, it's no longer a theory and becomes known.*

To give you an example, late in the morning on the first day, Rahasya asked fifteen of the thirty students to be counsellors and the other fifteen students to volunteer as clients. I raised my hand to be a client. He asked the fifteen counsellors to line up along the wall on the far side of the room. He instructed the fifteen clients to remain seated. He explained that we were about to do our first real counselling session, putting into practice what we had just learned. After the counsellors lined up along the wall, Rahasya asked the clients to walk over and select a counsellor for the individual session. Each of us walked over and selected a counsellor by simply standing in front of one of them.

The training we received that morning covered some basic things such as how the counsellor initially meets the client, how to greet and build rapport with a warm smile, and a welcoming nature. We also learned about the art of listening and how to create 'Heart Synchronicity'. To put this into practice, to learn the art of listening from the heart, Rahasya instructed the counsellors that for this short ten-minute session, the counsellor was not allowed to speak to the client at all, each counsellor was to listen from the heart.

He then added a twist; Rahasya said that for the entire length of the six-day counselling course, clients were to use 'real' issues. In other words, these were real counselling sessions and real life conflicts were to be explored in the sessions.

The session began with each client-counsellor pairing finding a bit of floor space to sit facing each other about a metre apart in the 'L' shaped legless chairs. This helps the client and counsellor to connect at the heart level.

My session started with a short meditation and then an interesting thing happened. My counsellor just looked into my eyes. I felt so much compassion and acceptance from her and I felt a tingling around my heart area. Feeling safe, I started talking, telling her about the cancer. After sharing only a few words, the waterworks started, tears streamed out of my eyes. It wasn't tears that I wanted to hide, these tears were different, they flowed out of me without any shame of showing my emotions to someone who was sitting right in front of me. The tears flowed effortlessly and I just allowed them to do so for the first time since I can remember. I was not ashamed of these tears, and although they were linked with the subject of my cancer, they were not sad tears at all, they were happy tears. They were beautiful tears that I allowed to happen.

It was clear that we were in this synchronistic heart state Rahasya had talked about. My counsellor and I were connected. She was feeling what I was feeling and tears started flowing out of her eyes as well. Ten minutes later Rahasya called us back to the main room where he invited us to share what we had experienced and what we had learned.

What do you attribute the crying to?

I was in a space where I felt safe, accepted, not judged by the person in front of me. Also I was willing to experience whatever happened. *As we explore ourselves, the space we create and our willingness to experience whatever is here, are two important components.* Sitting with my counsellor at the level of the heart, I started to let go. The resistance within me to avoid, escape and bury was no longer relevant, and after years of resisting my emotions and past experiences, the crying was a release, a release of what I had been holding onto. *As you let go, you move from resisting to allowing.* As I found out during this course, release naturally follows and there is nothing sad or bad about releasing long held tension. I called the tears happy tears, and happy tears happened regularly throughout this week.

Returning from lunch a couple of hours later, Rahasya initiated the second practical exercise. Keeping the same pairings, we held our second counselling session. This time the roles were reversed and I was the counsellor and the forty-year-old lady was the client.

Taking our seat at close proximity we had a short silent meditation. Then I was just there for her, without words, open, non-judgemental, unconditioned, listening and caring. The lady started telling me about the chronic-fatigue she had been suffering from for many years. She shared that her most recent relationship had just ended like all her other relationships ended, with her boyfriend suddenly walking out on her. She said it was due to her chronic-fatigue. She never had enough energy to leave her house, or enough energy to go out and be social with her boyfriend. As a result she always ended up alone and lonely. I felt what she was feeling and within thirty seconds of her sharing I started crying even though she was not crying. It was unexpected and very liberating to feel things, and to let my emotions go without controlling it.

Normally you don't cry?

In the past I rarely cried and never in front of others. Before the cancer, I don't remember crying at all because I had become numb to all the feelings and emotions that I didn't want to experience.

For the next four days of the course, Rahasya started each morning with a guided meditation. That was followed by an open reflective session where Rahasya invited anyone to come sit with him on the couch to share what they were experiencing or to ask questions that Rahasya would answer in relation to the course. This was followed by one to three hours of counselling training, and after that, we moved into exercises with at least two counselling sessions per day.

I really enjoyed the early morning reflective sessions run by Rahasya. Each of us were going deeper and deeper within ourselves during our daily counselling sessions, peeling back the layers in a kind of inner adventure. I learned a lot from what people shared of their own experiences – what they were feeling and coming to understand, and the huge shifts that were happening for people as a result of looking within with awareness.

Did you find the counselling sessions confronting?

No, all of this was new to me and I had no expectations or goals. However, I hadn't forgotten what the cells of my body had said to me. So, I was willing to experience without condition. In the first couple of days nothing dramatic or scary happened and I felt safe, so I relaxed more and more each day. I had no reservations about the counselling sessions, in fact it was the practical counselling sessions that held the power for me. No doubt this is why I ended up in that course, and the reason why some higher intelligence painted that picture of the tree covered road and the bright light at the end of the tunnel. Being here was exactly where I was meant to be at that time. Although I had no specific goals, it was a perfect environment to uncover the cause of my cancer. All of the students were open, supportive and compassionate. No matter what our story was or what happened in the past, it was met with compassion, understanding and love. So simple! Our stories were just stuff, some content of our life that stuck to us for whatever reason. It became very clear that our stories are not who we are. *Exploring ourself is the greatest gift we can give ourself.* As I was to find out, this was the gift of freedom itself.

Freedom?

Yes, freedom. Freedom from my inner conflicts. Freedom from all the things that had me resisting life. Inner freedom that is then experienced in our outer physical life. For me, the course itself turned out to be a process of letting go and discovering what is here. Each day I opened more and went deeper within, like peeling back layers of an onion. In most sessions tears flowed but there was no sadness, these tears were part of the healing. In the sessions I explored many topics, but the three topics I explored the most were cancer, my wife and my mother.

Each counselling session was revealing and as I progressed through a new layer of myself, I saw the truth through the falseness. Many issues came and went in quick succession, because most were superficial. On the surface they were minor things, or just symptoms of something else. As I came to allow, experience and see them without condition, they vanished no longer holding a power over me. It was like something was reaching inside me and turning my knob of tension from high to low. As each day passed, the tension within me slowly released.

On the third and fourth day of the course, I had a couple of sessions where the issue of Angelina, my mother and cancer came to the surface. What was revealed was that in relation to the cancer, Angelina was superficial and not the main issue. What also became crystal clear is that what happened with Angelina and my mother in America was also not the cause of the cancer. The things I thought caused my cancer were not the cause at all!

Really, then what caused the cancer?

At this point, I really had no clue what caused it. But I discovered fairly early on that my wife didn't cause it.

Over lunch on the third day I happened to sit with the assistant teacher Karima. I shared with her this revelation about my wife,

Peeling the onion brings happy tears

how I had explored my issues in the sessions, and how I had been blaming her for causing my cancer. I related how I found that these issues with my wife were superficial, and she was not the cause of the cancer. After some discussion, Karima explained that underneath all those superficial layers is the core, and I would know the core when I touched it.

The core?

Yes, she was talking about the core issue. The core issue is an inner conflict buried very deep within us, something we have great resistance to, something we never want to feel or experience again due to the acute pain and hurt associated with it. The core issue is commonly linked to the main theme in our life, that situation, drama or hurt reappearing over and over again. We hold onto this core issue through our resistance to it. It can be our greatest resistance. It is suppressed so deeply we have no idea what it is and often don't even know that it exists.

But as Karima says, when you touch the core with awareness, you will know it.

Karima also talked to me about relationships and what is really going on when there is a conflict and we feel triggered within the relationship. She introduced me to the concept of the mirror, explaining how our intimate partner is our biggest mirror to ourselves. Whatever we experience in the other, is really a reflection of ourselves. Rahasya explained this in a slightly different way when he said to me, *The other is only a situation showing you what you haven't met inside.*[R]

In other words, through our relationships, particularly our

interaction with our partner, the things that are hidden within us are revealed. We might move to blame the other for how we are feeling, but the other is just a mirror reflecting our self.

The other reflects our self?

Yes, 100%. When our partner does something that triggers us, we get angry for example. But this anger is not caused by our partner. We can only get triggered and angry if the source of that anger is already within us. In other words, if there was no anger in us, we wouldn't get angry with our partner, no matter what occurred. I found this very interesting, because up to this point I had been secretly blaming Angelina for lots of things in my life. In the days following my talk with Karima, I started looking more at myself as the possible cause of the disharmony I had been experiencing. In other words, I stopped blaming the mirror and I started taking responsibility for what was happening in my life. It didn't take long for me to see that the cause of my cancer was not 'out there.' the cause was 'right here,' in me!

But why would we want to cause our own cancer?

Consciously we would never want to create cancer or any illness for that matter. The problem is that many of us are not living consciously. When we live our life unconsciously, we easily end up resisting the very life we came here to experience, and unknowingly create the inner environment that leads to a situation like cancer.

Did Rahasya tell you that?

This was not something I was told this was something that I experienced. Rahasya pointed the way. He brought me to the door of awareness where I discovered this and more. Then on the morning of the fifth day of the course everything changed, and the most important discovery revealed itself to me.

~ 16 ~

Hallelujah,
I think I'm losing my mind

On the fifth day of the course, I awoke much earlier than normal. As I pulled myself out of bed, that open enthusiasm that had been with me all week was suddenly gone. Instead, there was a heavy cloud lingering in my head. The cloud was anxiety that came over me and I felt like running away.

I know the feeling. You have anxiety often?

No, I rarely experience anxiety, so this was unusual and very intense. To try and shake it off, I went for a walk on the beach, but that cloud in my head got heavier and heavier. I started jogging hoping to move the feeling out, but the anxiety stayed with me and my mind was screaming, "Get out of here!"

As I turned and started back up the beach, I saw something being tossed by the waves on the shoreline. The sunlight reflected off an object right into my eyes. I walked over, reached down and picked it up. It was a glass bottle covered in barnacles and green algae, with a cork sticking out of the top. Pulling the cork out I saw a rolled up piece of cardboard paper inside. I prised out the paper with a tiny stick and unfurled it to reveal its message. In the right hand corner of the paper was a picture of a bright golden sun with yellow rays shooting in all directions and underneath the sun were words written haphazardly all over the page which read:

Hallelujah, praise the lord

      Praise the lord, Hallelujah

   Hallelujah, praise the lord

 Hallelujah

      Hallelujah

   Hallelujah, praise the lord

Hallelujah?

You know, Hallelujah, an expression of rejoicing. Clearly I felt like I had nothing to rejoice in that moment. The anxiety I was experiencing was growing larger and darker and as a result I didn't think much of the message. I just put it in my back pocket and walked back up the beach towards Ninka's house.

The anxiety was such a weight on me I found it difficult to walk. As I came off the beach back over the sand dunes, my legs felt so heavy it took all of my concentration to step forward.

Ninka was her normal cheerful self, buzzing around the kitchen, making a juice, telling me a story. After returning to her house I hadn't said a word to her. She sensed something wasn't right and she stopped mid-sentence asking "What's wrong Steven, what's going on?"

I told Ninka that I wasn't going to Mevlana that day. I told her I couldn't go because I felt like I was losing my mind.

Ninka just gave me a big hug and said it would be all right. She tried to encourage me to come along to Mevlana. Before long it was time to go and she motioned for me to jump into the car. I didn't say a word and I didn't move from my seat in the kitchen.

Ninka gave me a kiss on the cheek, grabbed her keys and jumped into her Corolla. As she was backing out of the driveway, she stopped in the middle of the street, looked back at me and reached over and opened the passenger door. She sat there for a minute, waiting and looking at me with her big green eyes. Ignoring the voice inside of me that was screaming, "Run away!" I got up, dragged myself out and fell into the passenger seat.

~ 17 ~

Anxiety's wonderful news

We arrived at Mevlana late. The drive there was not pleasant. I kept saying to myself "I'm losing my mind … I'm losing my mind … hold it together … I'm losing my mind". At times when the car came to a stop, I reached for the door handle to escape, but somehow I stayed in the car. It was such an unusual experience. I had never felt like this before, so heavy and with no idea of what was going on.

I didn't want to fall back to my old habit of resistance, and run away from what was uncomfortable. This time the inner urge to escape was more acute. I wanted to crawl into a big hole where nobody could find me.

As we pulled into Mevlana, my legs became stiff as if the lower part of my body was frozen solid. Struggling to get my legs to move, I dragged myself into Mevlana where everyone was already sitting on the floor in meditation. We sat down in the back of the room.

As part of the morning routine following the meditation, Rahasya invited students to come sit with him on the couch and share what they were experiencing as part of the course and daily counselling sessions. Usually a number of hands shoot straight into the air to volunteer for the sharing, but this particular morning nobody raised their hand. As I looked around the room, I found myself sitting there with my hand raised as Rahasya pointed to me and called me up to the couch to speak with him.

As I sat on the couch, Rahasya handed me a microphone. He then turned and looked at me and said, "Welcome Steven, what's going on?"

I said: "I don't know, I've been going really well up until this morning. But today I feel so anxious, like there is a huge black cloud in my head. I didn't want to come here today, my legs didn't want to take me."

Rahasya replied, "Hallelujah, praise the lord!"

Hallelujah, praise the lord? Really, he said that?

Yes, I couldn't believe it either. Those exact words that were in the bottle! He had never said anything religious-sounding before. Those words were not part of his normal vocabulary since I had known him.

Rahasya then turned towards me and moved his face a little closer. Looking into my eyes he said calmly, "Steven, this is wonderful news … You Are Not Losing Your Mind!"

I fell back on the couch wondering how the hell he knew that I felt I was losing my mind?

Rahasya explained the anxiety I was feeling, saying that I was touching the core. He went on to explain that anxiety is just your brain, the rational mind that acts as a governor controlling what comes up into our consciousness. It is designed to do this in this situation so that what we have repressed doesn't come rushing up all at once and overwhelm us. As we bring consciousness within and touch the core, it is like an unopened can of coke that has been shaken up. The bubbles, like the tension held within the Pain Body, want to be released. In other words, the emotional pain held in our cells, wants to come up to understanding as the universe is always seeking to bring balance in all things. As we bring consciousness within, that lid, our mind, relaxes its grip and allows that tension within to be released.

He repeated to me that I was not going crazy, and emphasised that this was wonderful news!

He then asked what else happened that morning?

I shared with the group that I woke at five am and felt this anxiety so I went for a walk on the beach to try and clear it. As I was walking on the beach I found a bottle on the shore with a message in it."

As I was saying this, Rahasya cut me off: "A message in a bottle! What did it say?"

Everyone in the room sat up holding their breath in anticipation of the message.

I then told them it said: Hallelujah, praise the lord!

The entire room erupted in laughter and amazement. Everyone got the cosmic joke. The universe was having a bit of a laugh and sending me an important message at the same time. I knew that this was not a chance coincidence, but a synchronicity. The universe was speaking to me directly, telling me that what was happening was meant to be, telling me to relax, remain open and go with it.

As the laughter subsided, Rahasya confirmed yet again this great news; the anxiety I was experiencing was the mind governing what was coming up. He told me to try to relax and let it happen. He said that this is natural and it is nature's way.

This anxiety is natural?

All experiences provide feedback to us. If you investigate any experience, whether labelled anxiety or joy, what do you find? The experience is comprised of three main ingredients: Thoughts, Feelings and Sensations. The body is a great barometer, a wonderful feedback system. With the feeling of anxiety, I felt heavy, my legs became stiff and frozen, and 'I am losing my mind' was the repetitive thought. Experiences show us something about ourselves, and how we interpret what the experience is showing us can make the experience feel natural or unnatural.

Before I sat on the couch with Rahasya, I interpreted the anxiety as bad and wanted to crawl into a big hole where nobody could find me. In other words, I was in resistance, I wanted to escape the experience. After Rahasya explained that the anxiety is a natural part of the process where I was meeting myself and releasing a long-held core tension, I no longer wanted to escape the experience, I stepped past my resistance and saw that what I was feeling and sensing in the body was fine and natural. My thoughts around what my body was showing me, went from rejection to acceptance, and with this I relaxed into what was here.

Anxiety can be unnatural in our misunderstanding of it and resistance to it. Anxiety can be natural in our understanding and relaxing into the greater reason why it's here.

Awareness is the key in all of this. When we meet our experience with awareness, then the experience is natural and accepted. When we avoid and don't meet our experience, we misinterpret the situation, label it as unnatural, which leads to tension and further avoidance of what is here. This in itself is the story of resistance;

whatever you resist persists. That anxiety, the inner tension we avoid becomes a constant companion called ongoing suffering.

What happened when you relaxed with anxiety?

The anxiety faded away.

A lot of the anxiety I had been experiencing was due to my resistance to actually having anxiety, and the fear of not knowing what was happening. Once I understood what was happening I stopped resisting, and the related anxiety faded away.

After my talk with Rahasya I sat on a cushion on the floor in front of the couch hugging my knees as Rahasya gave his teachings for the day. My whole body started shaking. It was noticeable, and although I didn't understand the shaking, I just let go and let nature take its course, safe in the knowing I wasn't losing my mind.

This universe is intelligent, it brings to us exactly what we need at exactly the right moment, even when it's disguised as disease. To get the gift and its greater wisdom, we become still, curious and train the eyes to look beyond what is appearing on the surface of things. *Here now is the place of miracles.*

~ 18 ~

Meeting the Unknown

Did you find out what the core tension was?

It revealed itself in the counselling session that afternoon, and with it my life changed forever.

I stayed there on the floor at the foot of the couch while everyone went for lunch. My body shook like the rumbling volcano before it releases whatever is under its crusty skin.

An hour later everyone shuffled back into the room. Rahasya asked for fifteen volunteers to be counsellors and fifteen clients. I chose to be a client. The counsellors walked over and stood against the wall. Rahasya asked the clients to go and select a counsellor.

In the previous four days whenever I picked a counsellor, I always picked the same type of person, someone who looked soft, warm and welcoming. From across the room, I saw a lady who displayed these qualities so I walked towards her. Just metres away from her, one of the other clients slipped in front of me and stood in front of that lady counsellor, selecting her as their counsellor.

I stepped back and looked around and noticed that everyone had selected a counsellor already except me. Then I saw her, the one remaining counsellor. It was 'the crazy lady', the one who seemed so out-of-control angry, the same one I had heard screaming many times in the counselling sessions earlier that week. The entire week I had avoided her, never spoken to her or even made eye contact with her because she was so scary. Shit!

I walked over to her and stood in front of her. She didn't flinch. She didn't put out a hand to greet me, there was no smile or a word. She just stood there like a plastic mannequin staring straight into my eyes. Our faces were only a foot apart and with nowhere else to look I stared back into her emotionless eyes.

As I looked there, I saw an incredible toughness that was so different from all the other counsellors I had before. As she stared back at me like a rock, a thought filled my head, "She is tough enough, she can take it, go for it!"

She can take what?

She could handle whatever was at the core of me. I still didn't know what it was, this tension, this monster hidden within. Somehow I knew this woman could handle whatever it was.

We found a spot far away from everyone on the other side of the room. As I sat in front of her, she didn't change her faceless expression. After a short meditation I found myself talking about my mother.

I spoke for less than a minute and then suddenly my mouth locked shut and I couldn't speak. It was some kind of bodily reaction that I had no control over, like the day in the fifth grade when I started walking towards my teacher and froze in the middle of the room not allowing myself to ask for help. Here I was again at the summit within myself, freezing in-place due to something inside me that habitually demands the avoidance of the unknown hurt part of me. This freezing was a last ditch resistance of the thinking mind.

But weren't you allowing it to happen, after Rahasya spoke to you, you said you relaxed and allowed it?

Yes, consciously I was relaxing and allowing, but the mind was in a state of negotiating, governing the situation. This was big, the core conflict that I had habitually escaped all my life. My interpretation is that there was a silent negotiation going on, and while that was happening, my mouth froze shut.

Who was negotiating what?

The best way I can explain it is that conscious awareness and the thinking mind (the Ego) were working things out. Rahasya says *the mind only needs to relax a little bit for a big shift to happen.*[R] What Rahasya told me on the couch that morning was enough for the mind to relax just enough, to allow the very thing that had been habitually resisted for thirty years to be here now.

Awareness is a higher power than thought; and the mind is just a bundle of thoughts.[R] So through conscious awareness and a willingness to be with whatever is here, the mind lets go and allows where it had been resisting. In this letting go, what had been resisted is revealed, bringing a new understanding and an instant shift in perspective.

What was revealed?

For five minutes my jaw was locked shut and my entire body became stiff like a board. But as the minutes ticked by, that stone-like crazy lady in front of me softened, her eyes became full of compassion and our hearts connected in a synchronistic bond. I witnessed her tough exterior becoming soft. But I was stuck in my moment of truth with my old friend resistance and her heels were dug in deep. My counsellor somehow knew what was happening, and she held the space for me, making it safe for me to open up. She spoke to me, trying to draw me out, trying to get me past that final gate of resistance. She said, "Steven, tell me about your mother. She is a nurse, someone who gives of herself to others … Tell me, what does she look like?" My jaw relaxed, I let go completely.

Speaking softly I started describing my mother. Yes, she is a nurse, a cardiac care nurse who worked in the heart unit of a hospital just outside of Boston. She is a wonderful person, so giving and caring; she always cared so much for us kids … she cares more for us than she cares for herself. Love … Love was always there. And …

As I was describing my mother I froze again because a vivid image flooded my senses. It was an image of a massive rubber band that was 1 metre wide (3 feet). The rubber band was stretched to 3 metres long (10 feet), stretched so much that it was breaking into strands in the middle. At each end of the rubber band were two forces that were pulling it in opposite directions. LOVE was pulling in one direction and ANGER was pulling in the opposite direction. I was the rubber band, this was a picture of me, and I was stretched to breaking point by the opposing forces of Love and Anger.

I knew instantly that this was directly related to the cancer. It was anger, anger that I buried under my skin never to be seen again. It was anger that I had held down within me, that I never allowed myself to feel, express or experience. It was anger that I repressed so much I didn't even know I had it.

The cause of my cancer was unrealised anger! Yet, even though I buried my anger never to be felt again, the burying of anger didn't get rid of it. That anger never left me, it remained very much alive within me. *Unexpressed anger is an energetic entity that can be a very self-destructive force.*

Love was pulling in the opposite direction because although anger towards my mother was there, love for her was also there in strength. In the fifth grade it was fear of hurting my mother, the person I loved unconditionally, that prevented me from handing the note to my teacher.

So there was a battle between Love and Anger?

Yes, you could put it that way. Anger was there, but because of the love I had for my mother, I felt that I didn't have the right to feel angry towards her. From an early age, anger was something I decided was bad and therefore I wouldn't allow it, I held anger within to get rid of it so I would never experience it. That buried anger grew stronger inside as it remained unexpressed all of my life until Mevlana. Anger was my biggest resistance. I refused to allow myself to feel anger towards someone I loved. Over time, I tricked myself into believing that the anger didn't exist, yet it was there, eating away at me the entire time.

You are saying Anger is not bad?

No emotion is a bad emotion as long as it is expressed … appropriately.

Looking back, it is no surprise that my inner conflict between Love and Anger turned into cancer. Resisting the anger that was a part of me, due to the love that was a part of me, was 'me fighting me', the invisible form of what doctors often refer to as cancer – 'the body attacking itself.'

My resistance to allowing anger was so inbred, that it took cancer, the risk of losing my life, to finally step past resistance and allow the anger to be there. *Cancer is a situation that asks us to put ourselves first, an opportunity to love all parts of ourselves.*

In seeing and understanding the image of the rubber band, I sat there for some time witnessing and welcoming the anger that was here. I didn't try to get rid of it or do anything with it. I simply allowed, watched and experienced the anger, feeling it as sensations in my body. *In meeting what we have been resisting, there is nothing we need to do but experience it.* As I experienced anger my entire body began to shake. The tension inside felt like an explosive bomb ready to go off, particularly in the area of my lower belly where the cancer was, the same place that the Pain Body of anger was located.

My body was shaking and trembling and then it happened, an inner volcanic explosion. The cells in the lower part of my body, near the base of my spine and lower stomach area shook, rumbled and then opened up. I felt the cells in and around where I had cancer open in an explosive release of energy, and I felt that energy rise up within me. The energy went from the base of my spine, up my spine through my stomach, through the solar plexus, up through my heart area, through my neck and throat, up and out the top of my head. As the energy left the top of my head, I felt it encompass my entire body, floating and encircling me like a loving embrace.

At the same time memories came bubbling up and I knew what was behind the anger. I saw myself back at my house in the woods of New England arriving home from school on that special day in the fifth grade, the day I didn't hand in the note to my teacher and grew a thick skin. I saw myself pulling the note out of my pocket and looking at it one last time as I threw the note into the waste basket. In the counselling session I read those five words loud and clear to my counsellor: "My mother is an alcoholic". I finally expressed what went unexpressed for 30 years.

I felt relieved and somewhat elated in the simple understanding of what I had been resisting, a sense of freedom in seeing what was behind the cause of my cancer. I can't emphasis this enough, to simply see and understand what the unseen hurt was, was one of the greatest gifts. That hidden unconscious part of me was now fully conscious. The answer had been within me all the time. There was no more wondering what the tension inside was, and soon I would find there was never any more pain relating to this core issue.

Little did I know that in that very moment of meeting and experiencing anger, the Pain Body of anger that was the cause of my cancer released and dissolved. The energetic entity behind the cancer was no longer and my cancer was cured in that instant.

Through the process of allowing and being here with the unknown, the unknown becomes seen and understood. With understanding, truth and healing follows.

As I shared those five words with my counsellor, a flood of happy tears flowed from our eyes. Understanding what it was, she reached out and grabbed my hands and said, "Steven, this is also my core issue. It is the issue I have been struggling with all my life and never been able to understand until right now. Thank you, thank you, thank you so much!" As it turned out, she had also grown up in an alcoholic household, with no stability in her upbringing, feeling abandoned by her father, feeling her childhood had been taken away and had unknowingly suppressed her anger inside. We were meant to come together in this moment and both of us were healed.

With thirty minutes still to go in this counselling session, we sat there, both of us crying happy tears, with a strange funny laughter sneaking in every now and then.

I was meeting anger for the first time. That part of me that I had denied and denounced most of my life. Anger was now allowed to be here, no longer disowned like the black sheep of the family, it was welcome home. As I sat with my counsellor, I felt a life force surged through my body. *On the other side of anger is vitality.*[R]

My counsellor and I didn't talk for the remainder of the session we just let this experience unfold. Inwardly, I saw my mother before my eyes and my whole perception of her changed. I could see her from different angles, from above, from the side and all around. And I could see her from her very own perspective as it relates to alcoholism. A story came forward of her own youth, one that I had long forgotten. She was born in Hectors Creek, a poor desolate area in the back woods of North Carolina. She was the youngest daughter of four children. She had two sisters and one brother. Soon after she was born, her father died in a car accident. Her mother was very poor, stuck in a situation with no money, no husband and four kids all under the age of eight to take care of. Not being able to cope with the situation, her mother ran away, leaving her kids in a tiny house in the woods of North Carolina. At that time my mother was four years old. Many months passed before the authorities found them and they were literally starving to death. My mother had been abandoned by her own mother.

After the children were discovered they were put into an orphanage in Charlotte, North Carolina, where my mother lived until the age of eighteen. My mother told that because she was so malnourished upon arriving to the orphanage, the kitchen staff took her into the kitchen after every meal to give her a second serving to try and bring her back to health. This went on for many years.

Growing up in the orphanage was tough, and she said she never felt loved. She told me how excited all the orphan children got at Christmas time because they would receive the only present of the year, a single orange. To her, life was about survival. She shared a core belief that in life you must fight to survive. She felt she had to fight for everything or be swept under the carpet. She was, and still is, a survivor. But she could never come to terms with being abandoned by her mother, a child who grew up without love. Those memories of the orphanage haunted her. She would never talk about her inner clouds, and like me, she just shut them out, grew a thick skin and buried it all and eventually turned to the bottle to avoid the pain inside.

As I looked at this from this new perspective, it became clear that she drank alcohol to cope with her past, memories, feelings and hurts. This was her way to avoid her own inner pain. She was no different than me trying to avoid what was inside, not realising that those hurts don't go away in our resistance to them, but eventually catch up with us. Each time it caught up with her, she drank more and more to escape. Soon it turned into alcoholism – a constant need to avoid her self.

As I sat there in this session with my counsellor in a state of awareness, I realised that my mother's alcoholism was not meant to harm me, she was simply trying to cope, she was doing the best she could to survive and she knew of no other way. She didn't mean to emotionally abandon me. She didn't mean to hurt me in any way. She was doing the best she could in the circumstances. The truth is quite the opposite of what I had been telling myself. In fact, none of what happened was about me. The story I had been telling myself all these years, the story of abandonment and betrayal, the story that I wasn't good enough and a victim, it was completely untrue. It was just a story that I made up from a very young age as I was not capable of understanding what was happening with my mother and my family. And it's interesting because ***it is the nature of the mind that it can't tell the difference between a thought and reality.***[R] So that's how it went from an early age, the story I told myself, made of the thoughts in my mind, became my reality.

Yes, but she was an alcoholic and that had a big effect on you.

It was not my mother's alcoholism that caused my crisis, it was my resistance to that situation that caused my suffering and eventually led to cancer. For my mother, it was not the fact she was abandoned by her mother and grew up in an orphanage that caused her problems, it was her resistance to that situation that was the problem: the use of alcohol to avoid pain. *Whatever we resist follows us like an uninvited shadow. All we need to do is invite it home and rejoice at its arrival.*

The counselling session ended. As I stood up from my seat, I felt physically lighter. It was as if the thousand pound gorilla that had been on my back all my life was suddenly gone. As I stepped back into the main room, I seemed to glide across the floor. That heaviness that had always been a part of me was gone. I was feeling on top of the world, light as a feather, so alive and vital, and love was exploding out of me. Like a battery that had gone flat, that energy behind anger that had been held captive inside no longer had any power behind it. As anger dissipated, love expanded. The other students sensed what was happening and they all ran up and hugged me and stood around me like bugs drawn to the light in the night. It was love that drew them in.

As I walked through the door to the courtyard I met Rahasya coming in the other way. I said, "Rahasya, I uncovered the core, the big enchilada!" He smiled genuinely and congratulated me on this wonderful news. It was no surprise to him that I had experienced what he has witnessed many times before. In meeting myself with awareness, the unknown became known, what was false was no longer, the power behind the disharmony went flat, and I was healed at the level of the mind and the body followed.

~ *19* ~

Our story is never the truth!

Wow, that is quite a story. So awareness fixes us?

Lily, there is nothing we need to 'fix.' There is nothing wrong with us. It is simply our own misunderstanding that causes our ongoing disharmony. Awareness brings a higher perspective, a new understanding, and a truth that re-contextualizes our misunderstandings.

What was your misunderstanding that caused cancer?

Well, I was just a young boy and certain emotional experiences were happening in my life. We all have experiences. Experiences are not the problem, it's what we do with our experiences that counts.

The first misunderstanding was that I wrongly blamed myself for the situation that was happening around me. When in fact, what was going on with my mother had absolutely nothing to do with me.

My mother and I have always been very close. As a young boy I saw how much she was suffering. I naturally wanted to take away all of her pain so she would be happy, and in no way did I want to give her any more pain. In my mind at that crucial moment in the fifth grade when I was reaching out for help, I pulled back thinking my mother would get in trouble or be confronted in some way which might bring her more pain. It's not uncommon that our dedication and love for others is stronger than the dedication and love we have for ourselves. As a child I didn't understand what was happening with my mother, and the only logical conclusion I could come up with was to point the finger at myself. So I unconsciously blamed myself, thinking the only reason she would abandon me and turn to alcohol was because I wasn't good enough. I eventually came to this wrong conclusion, and that followed me throughout my life. So the first misunderstanding was that I blamed myself for the situation that had nothing to do with me.

The second misunderstanding I had was that I needed to bury and avoid the painful experiences that were happening. In other words, my strategy to survive was to become unconscious. *Unconsciousness is the denial of experience.*[R] So, my second misunderstanding was that becoming unconscious was a great solution.

By becoming unconscious to the pain, I thought I was getting rid of those painful things I didn't want, expecting that they would no longer be part of my life. But the outcome was the exact opposite. In the denial of my hurt, I kept the conflict alive and carried it around with me wherever I went. Over time it grew and became suffering, the thousand pound gorilla on my back.

The third misunderstanding had to do with the interpretation of my entire childhood. The 'story of me' that I created and held onto for 30 years was that I was a victim, betrayed and emotionally abandoned by the person in my life who I considered to be the very source of love. Through this misunderstanding I created a false story and believed it to be true. As our heart felt beliefs become our reality, this 'story of me' affected everything in my life that followed.

Whatever experience occurs in our life, we automatically form an interpretation around the events that take place. In our resistance to certain experiences, our interpretation is never the truth.

Our interpretation is never the truth?

I know this is hard to believe, but please investigate this for your self. When you experience a situation that is hurtful, the habitual reaction of most people is to resist it. We deny the experience which is the very definition of unconsciousness. We unknowingly lock away an interpretation of the experience as we are denying it. The interpretation you lock away, ***the story you create when you are in a state of unconsciousness is never the truth.***[R] When we are not in resistance to an experience, there is no conflict, we become present and allow it, and the story you create when you are in a state of consciousness is sourced from truth.

Here, let me say it a slightly different way. As we shut down around a challenging situation we don't want to see, feel or fully experience, we simultaneously form an interpretation of that experience. We form an interpretation AS we shut our eyes to it. In our resistance to it, we lock in the energy along with our story of the experience. The problem is that our interpretation is never true. Think about it, how could our interpretation be accurate if it was formed when we are closed and not looking?

Yes, keep going.

The mind is quite incredible, but please realise that *our mind is a story creation machine,* [R] and the stories we tell ourselves with eyes shut are the kindling that feed our disharmony.

It is the nature of the mind that it cannot distinguish between a thought and reality. A story is simply thoughts from the past that we replay in our mind. Like a favourite movie that we watch again and again, we carry around our stories and we replay them habitually. In this way, the story becomes our reality. And because our story becomes our reality, we defend our stories passionately. This is one of the challenges and opportunities of a life threatening illness, because even with something like cancer staring us in the face, we can be so identified and attached to our stories, that we become rigid and defend them even to the point of our own physical demise. *Part of the opportunity with cancer is to stop defending our stories and see them through the impartial eyes of awareness.* Here the false fades away and the truth is revealed.

How did seeing past your story heal you?

In that final counselling session, through the eyes of awareness I saw the truth from the false story I had created in my mind. I brought consciousness to what had been unconscious for 30 years, and as a result the truth was revealed, misunderstanding resolved and healing naturally followed.

Yes, but how did the healing happen, what happened?

You could say that it happens in the same way light is brought into a dark room. The misunderstanding is that darkness exists. Can you shine a darkness torch into a bright room and make it dark? No. The darkness doesn't exist. If a room is dark, there is nothing but an absence of light. Introduce light (truth) to the room that was absent of light, and suddenly it has light.

It is the same with our unresolved conflicts and Pain Bodies. We have tension, accumulated emotional pain, a darkness *that is nothing but an absence of truth.* We hold onto stories from the past that we believe to be true. We play the stories over and over again, and as our mind considers them to be real, they become our reality. But in fact they are just false stories, created in a state of unconsciousness, at times in our life that we denied our experience.

Our stories are only misunderstandings that get solidified due to our ongoing resistance. Like a room absent of light, these misunderstandings can only exist in the absence of the truth. As we become consciously aware and meet ourselves, truth enters and the false disappears.

In this same way, the Pain Body of anger that was behind my cancer dissolved the moment I met the anger and experienced it in a state of consciousness. The misunderstandings I supported for over 30 years in the denial of my experience, could not exist with the truth that entered in a state of awareness. Where my eyes had been shut, they were now open, seeing the truth through the eyes of consciousness. *Truth is the healer that shifts the mind, and the body follows the mind.*

The great India master Sri Nisargadatta Maharaj, puts it succinctly this way:

We are slaves to what we do not know;
*   of what we know we are masters.*

Whatever vice or weakness in ourselves,
*   we discover and understand its causes and its workings,*
*   we overcome it by the very knowing;*

The unconscious dissolves when brought into the conscious.

Truth is the healer. There is nothing that needs fixing inside of us, there are only misunderstandings. One moment with truth and our misunderstanding shifts and everything changes.

In my final counselling session my consciousness shifted as I brought awareness to what had remained unconscious within me for 30 years. Like a light entering a dark room, the truth behind my false stories were revealed, my point of view naturally shifted and the Pain Body, the energetic entity behind my symptom of cancer literally dissolved.

Why did it dissolve?

Bring awareness and truth to any story, and the untruths, the energy behind what is false dissolves because it is only an absence of truth. What is false simply can't exist in the light of the truth. Or to put it another way, **when we see what is true, the false stops.**[R]

So if I bring consciousness inside, my cancer will be cured?

Living consciously and bringing awareness to what is here right now is definitely a brilliant recipe for living. Awareness is a state, an environment that enables shifts in consciousness to happen, and a shift in consciousness will change all aspects of your life including your physical health. Will it cure cancer? I am a living example. However, I suggest that you experiment without any fixed goals. With awareness, we are not doing, we are simply being with what is here. Goals are mind oriented, so to have goals strengthens the mind that tries to keep a lid on everything. The mind by its very nature is resistant and is comfortable in the past and the future, but doesn't understand 'being with what is here right now'. What I am talking about here is beyond the mind. Awareness by its very nature is beyond the mind. Awareness is a state of impartial witnessing. So what I am suggesting is that you bring awareness to what is here and witness what happens. We uncover ourselves, those parts we have forgotten by stepping beyond the thinking mind. This is why Rahasya uses meditation and other techniques, they help us become present, aware, to be here right now, and to step beyond the layers of the mind. *Here now is the place where miracles happen.*

So ... no guarantees?

My own experience is an example of how cancer and other disharmonies can be healed forever. We can prepare ourselves, create the environment that enables healing, but as with everything there is an element of grace. Awareness is a state that is naturally receptive and grace finds you when you are receptive, open to receive.

It is now over sixteen years since that fateful day at Mevlana and

I have maintained regular checkups with my doctors. The medical fraternity has declared me completely cured of cancer and there was no reoccurrence and no side effects, except for the positive side affects of the ending of my longstanding inner disharmony. This permanent cure is not a result of the operation that allowed me to survive, but the result of meeting and healing the energetic hurt which led to cancer. The cure came spontaneously on the fifth day at Mevlana.

Healing the cause of our conflict starts on the inside and is then reflected in our outer physical life. And although I can't give you a guarantee, I can point you in the right direction by sharing Rahasya's telling words: ***Where there is a shift of consciousness, spontaneous healing can and often happens.***[R]

~ 20 ~

The elements are:
Presence and Love

Your healing happened so fast. I don't know if I really believe this is possible for me?

Everyone is unique and every healing can be equally unique. In some ways my healing happened really fast, but in other ways it took over 30 years and a very confronting situation for me to allow it to happen. At the precipice I was lucky or perhaps destined to meet someone like Dr. Rahasya Kraft who showed me the way. With these elements coming together, the healing happened quickly. Healing can truly happen in an instant, and I feel that this has more to do with the mechanics of the universe than it does with miracles. What I see with the people I meet, and what my story shows, is that we are the ones blocking our own road to health and happiness. As soon as we let go and become receptive, the entire universe gets behind us to guide us and bring us back into balance. Harmony is the nature of this universe, not malignancy. But being human means we have the means to make decisions about our life and can choose to live consciously or unconsciously. We are the ones who build a fence around ourselves, and we are the ones who hold the key that unlocks the door. *We have to be very creative to create a state of ill health.*

If we block ourselves, what allowed you to remove these blocks and heal?

If I had to narrow it down to two things, it would be Presence and Love. The unconditional love connection with my kids fuelled my desire to live. I made my desire for life clearly known to the universe. At the precipice, the love for myself gave me a willingness to let go of a lifetime of resisting, where I became receptive and willing to be here now, regardless of any outcome. The unfolding of the course with Rahasya and the love I felt from my fellow students during that course supported me greatly. It really was a space of love at Mevlana, and each counselling session was held in a safe and loving space allowing me to open and explore what I had not explored before. Being there in a state of presence is the opposite of what I had been doing all my life. Rahasya taught me about consciousness, reminding me how to be present – in that state I moved from 'doing' to being here with What Is. Through meditation I allowed everything to be as it is and became one with the moment. Through presence we can bypass the gates of the thinking mind and its resistances.

What about after the course, were there any lasting effects?

After the course I stayed at Ninka's house for two days. I needed a bit of time to assimilate what had happened. My body was feeling light, and my psyche was feeling delicate and loving. To honour the shift of consciousness that was still happening, I stayed quiet, remained mainly alone, went for long walks on the beach and sat in contemplation. I remember Ninka inviting me out for breakfast on the morning after the course finished. She was meeting a group of friends at a popular cafe in Byron Bay. She wanted me to come and share my story of what had happened during the course with her friends. Feeling delicate, I didn't want to be with large groups of people at the time. That last counselling session opened me to the core while at the same time releasing a long held tension, and although I felt incredible, clear and physically light, I was in a very raw natural state.

What was happening?

I was experiencing the authentic me, the 'me' that had been shut down and covered over for such a long time. Also my consciousness had shifted and with such a shift in perception it can take a little while for that new reality to fully integrate into our mind and body.

I didn't go out for breakfast and remained quiet and kept to myself. A few days later I flew home to my family in Sydney. I arrived home in a heightened state of love and gratitude for them and for everything. Angelina and I came together like never before physically and emotionally. It was love that now naturally pulled me forward, and anger was no longer pulling me the other way.

I had always seen my kids through the eyes of unconditional love and now I was seeing Angelina in the same way. I experienced love in a new way where all those things that had tainted my vision no longer dimmed my view of her. I imagined it was like coming home after being kidnapped for a long period of time, because in many ways our resistance to life holds us to ransom. It holds us in the dark, it dims our view and keeps us from experiencing the truth.

So no side effects from the course?

There were many side effects and they were all positive. My heart was open and I had uncovered the authentic part of myself. The inner clouds that had been my constant companion were gone exposing a vast inner sky, a 'me' that was infinite, endless love.

How did you know it was a total healing at Mevlana?

Rahasya told me that you can tell if your Pain Body is healed when you no longer get triggered by similar events that triggered you in the past. The opposite is also true, you can tell if there is something that needs healing if you get triggered by experiences that happen in the present.

Your reactions to life events hold the key. If you get triggered during life's situations, if you get angry, point fingers, shout, call people names, feel anxious or stressed, feel tension in the body, run away, turn to drugs, alcohol or food as a means of escape, this is what I call a 'trigger'. This points to something that needs investigation and healing.

Often we point fingers and blame whatever is in front of us when we get triggered. This is why intimate relationships fall apart, because the hurt inside us that gets triggered is projected onto our partner and we think they are the problem. If we get triggered, the issue is not 'out there' it is 'in here'. We can't feel angry unless anger is already inside, a part of us. The trigger appears as a signpost telling us that there is something within us that needs to be met.

You had this kind of proof with your healing?

Yes. A few months after leaving Mevlana, I flew to America to visit my parents. In the days after Mevlana I thought of my father and wanted to spend some time with him and my mother. I just wanted to say to him in person that I loved him, something I hadn't done since my childhood. So I flew to Florida to see my parents.

I could always read the state of my mother, I only needed to hear her speak two words and I knew if she was sober or intoxicated. In person or on the phone 30,000 miles away, two words was all it took. And throughout my life up until this point, whenever I heard my mother in an intoxicated state, it triggered me instantly. My body would become tense and I would feel a charge within my belly.

So an interesting thing occurred on the trip back to Florida. As the plane landed in Tampa, I felt very relaxed, whereas on previous trips I would tense up in anticipation of seeing my mother, unconsciously wanting to avoid the pain that was buried within me.

I rented a car and drove to my parents' house. I arrived and knocked on their front door. Nobody answered. I opened the door and walked in. From the other side of the house I heard my mother say a long slow, "S T E V E E E E !" In that instant I knew she was intoxicated.

For the first time for as far as I could remember, I didn't get triggered. I felt no charge within me, my belly didn't get tense, and

I didn't want to turn and run. I felt fine, walked over and gave them both incredible loving hugs.

To this day, that tension and hurt linked to this common theme of my life never returned. This is the sign of complete and total healing.

What about the ongoing relationship with your wife, mother and mother in-law? Did the events in Mevlana have any affect on this?

The intense hurts I felt over the events that happened in America with Angelina and my mother and then back in Australia with Angelina and my mother-in-law, were not because of their actions, those were hurts that were already inside of me. The interplay between my mother, mother in-law and Angelina were just the situations that triggered the hurt that was already there, mirroring where I was at internally.

On the fifth day of the counselling course at Mevlana, that hurt dissolved as I became one with it. So to answer your question, the relationship with my mother, mother in-law and Angelina came into harmony after returning from Mevlana. The Pain Body, that is, the unrealised anger, had been experienced, and I saw the truth behind all the events that took place in America and on the farm in Australia. As a result there were no remaining issues. Love now pulled me forward and my anger was gone. Angelina and I went into a deeper state of realised Love. My relationship with my mother grew to become one of total non judgemental acceptance. The love we already shared remains, and I am at complete peace with her with no hidden anger. On my next trip to the farm, I felt more welcomed by Anna than ever before. Our connection grew to a place where I no longer felt like her son in-law, but like her very own son. Oh and by the way, my mother has been sober for over 15 years now on her own account.

So regarding the proof of my complete and total healing, you could say that the medical 'all clear' is the 'physical' sign, whereas the great shifts in my relationships and not getting triggered anymore around my mother's drinking are the 'invisible' signs. Both signs are of equal importance in complete and total healing.

The key to knowing if something is healed is to look for the signs. You just live your life and at some point you will end up back in a situation that previously triggered you. Just observe what is here, observe your emotions and your physical body reactions. If you get triggered and that charge lasts, that is simply a call for inner inquiry. With awareness, you can meet and heal it.

~ 21 ~

You can 'Change your mind'

Lily, my taxi arrives in an hour and I sense you have some questions.

> Yes, I have questions about my cancer and how what you are saying directly relates to me.

OK, ask away.

> What about chemotherapy? My doctor has already talked to me about chemotherapy and his plan to use it in my treatment. Friends and family are giving me conflicting advice about this. I am in two minds about chemotherapy, so I wonder if you had chemotherapy and can you tell me what you think about it?

Chemotherapy is an important consideration as it is so widely used in mainstream medicine today. I personally didn't have chemotherapy or radiotherapy treatment.

> Should I use it?

This is a very personal decision, and I am not here to give you advice on what specific medical treatment is right for you.

But I just don't know and am confused.

Yes, I understand. But I really can't tell you what is right for you because I am not you. You are unique and the solution that is right for you is also unique. This is why it is important for you to tune in to yourself. You are the best person to know what is right for you. We have learned to look outside ourselves and ask others what is best for us, but nobody knows us better than we know ourselves. In spite of this we tend to believe others before we believe ourselves. It just takes a small shift to start looking inwards instead of looking outside of our selves for the answers.

One of the most important things I want to share with you today is to *listen to and trust yourself*. If you are in a state of ill-health or any form of disharmony, then tuning in and trusting yourself is important, because as you become present and tune in, you connect with the universe and the wisdom within. As you become aware and tune in, you can come to know what is right for you.

Each of us is unique in many ways, such as in our physical makeup, in our past experiences and conditioning, in our willpower and our purpose in life. As a result, the solution to bring balance and health to our situation is equally unique. Not everyone on the planet fits into a square hole, the hole that often the medical system tries to put us through due to the sheer number of people it must deal with, and the limited time and resources it has. I am not putting down the medical system in any way, it simply is what it is, but it is a system that has to deal with a lot of people and thus must find a standardised repeatable solution. I feel it is important that you don't relinquish your responsibility in making decisions or finding the right solution. Don't relinquish it to your doctor, to your family or to your friends and colleagues. Take an active leading role at all times and direct the whole thing. Those other people may care for you, but they are not living in your skin, they don't know the real you. Their antenna will not be as finely tuned into the radio station called 'you' as you will be, especially in this time of crisis. Become present and trust your inner guidance.

But what if they disagree with what I feel is right for me?

You might get your own indication, call it a strong feeling, instinct or an intuition if you like, that you should follow a certain course of action at a time when a family member or a doctor is pushing you in another direction. They might tell you that you are wrong if you don't agree with them because from their reality they can only see things in a certain way. To this I say 'tune in and trust yourself.'

It is easy to get confused by all the advice you get by everyone around you. Find that quiet space, use the tools of meditation to quiet the thinking mind, calm the chaos and tune into the wellspring of intelligence to find out what is right for you. Follow your instincts and that first gut feeling. Your first instinct is what comes in before the rational mind takes over and analyses to the point where we doubt ourselves. With so many people speaking in our ears, it is easy to fall into 'analysis paralysis' where we can end up chasing our own tail.

It can be easy and tempting to just give your decisions away, to just turn the responsibility over to some surgeon and 'be done with it'. Stay tuned-in because even when you follow the medical path, you need to be steering the ship, listening for the clues and making your own decisions. Trust and work with your surgeon if you are in an emergency situation and that path feels right to you, but continue to steer the ship. We are connected to the source of all answers. *Right now is the time to listen to and honour your self.* Yes, you are ready.

But my doctor wants an answer by Monday!

I know, cancer is a confronting situation that often accelerates self-discovery. *There is no time like the present to be present!*

I went to a meditation night being run by Rahasya recently and he talked about this very subject. He said that it can be very scary to turn inwards, to listen and trust our own inner voice, because there is no guarantee, there is no safety, and there is no reassurance ... but there is life!

He said that in our childhood consciousness, we still think that other people know better than that which calls from within us. And that which calls from within is the presence that we are, the intelligent response to now. **The true answers to any life problem arises from a silent moment from within, when the time is right, and the time is always now.**[R]

He added that if we try to skip ahead and bypass this moment, we suffer. If we are present in the unfolding of this moment, there is a creative flow. His advice was to be present, tune into yourself and do whatever you can in this moment from that space, then relax into the next step which is not revealed yet, until it is.

Experiment with this tonight when you go to bed. As you

lie in bed in silence, hold an intention of getting clarity about chemotherapy. Close your eyes and just witness whatever is here. You don't need to reject any thoughts, sensations, or feelings that come. Just be with whatever is there in the moment.

What is right for you can come in many different ways. It might come within a meditation as a thought, a vision, words you hear inside or a sensation in the body. It might come in your day-to-day life when you are walking your dog in the park for example. Be observant because a communication might come in a way you are not expecting. For example, in a chance meeting with someone who says something to you and suddenly everything clicks. Or perhaps in a song you hear on the radio that has a hidden message for you. As we live with awareness we become more observant of all the little things in life that we normally filter out and ignore. The Universe will send messages, and as we remain watchful we can pick up the signal. Particularly at this time when cancer is here, your senses will likely be heightened. But as with all times, you are connected to the source of all answers, the information is being broadcast on a special radio wave that is meant just for you. You are the best person in the world to tune into that wave and tailor a solution just right for you.

You make it sound so easy, but I don't know how to start.

The best place to start is to take the first step, experiment, and see what happens. There is nothing to lose by taking a step, but there is a lot to be gained.

But Steven my husband is telling me that chemotherapy is the only way to go.

Yes, that is a belief many have, and there are others who say it is the wrong way to go. It can be right for some and not right for others. Everyone has an opinion and the funny thing about opinions is that the only opinion that really matters is your own.

There is an incredible intelligence that surrounds you and is you. It is the same intelligence that created this universe, and instructs your body to take a breath even when you are in deep sleep. Could the intelligence that created this universe ever make a mistake? If you look at the complexity, the depth and the beauty of everything, from the deepest planets in far away galaxies, to the simple beauty of an unfolding flower on a spring morning. Could there be any lack of intelligence in our cells, made of the very same conscious matter as the galaxies and the flower? That intelligence is always with us.

What is more important than the chemotherapy question is what your inner guidance system is telling you. If you believe chemotherapy is right for you, then go with it. There is power behind your beliefs, so follow that inner guidance, provided you investigate those beliefs in the silent space beyond the thinking mind.

> Yes, I hear you, but I am in a dire situation right now, I don't have time to find this presence thing right now. I don't know if chemo is right for me or not!

Lets try a little experiment. Close your eyes for a moment. Take some long deep conscious breaths. Let all thoughts drift away and your body relax. Keep on breathing. And lets sit in silence for a few minutes. *[5 minutes pass]*

I am going to ask you a question and let me know the first thing that comes to you in any shape or form such as images, words, symbols, colours, feelings in the body, a smell or something else. Nothing may come and that is just fine too.

The question is: Would chemotherapy treatment be beneficial to Lily for healing her cancer? *[Silence for one minute]*

Can you share with me what you see and are experiencing?

I saw a green light appear, flash and then disappear.

How did it feel, how do you interpret the green light?

Green means go, like a green traffic light.

So in regards to chemotherapy, what meaning do you give to the green traffic light?

Go, I should have chemotherapy.

OK, lets stay in silence for a little while *[5 minutes pass]*
Has anything else come to you that you'd like to share?

No, nothing else.

OK, take a deep breath, come back now, gently stretch your body and wiggle your toes. And in your own time open your eyes.
Welcome back.
How do you feel Lily?

Relaxed, like I just had a nap.

That was just a little experiment and you can try that yourself tonight. In relation to chemotherapy you were shown the green light. And you know Lily you can relax with whatever path you take because nothing is set in stone, life is fluid not fixed. As you remain aware, you may get more guidance that takes you in another direction. As Rahasya suggests, do whatever you can in this moment, then relax into the next step which is not revealed yet, until it is.

I will try. Thank you.
    I feel the truth in what you are saying about how emotions can cause disease. Do you know of anyone who has proven this?

I have followed a German Doctor over the years who has worked with thousands of patients in a leading medical institution in Germany. His life's work is one example.

Really, who is this doctor?

His name is Dr. Ryke Geerd Hamer. His life's work is known as Germanic New Medicine. Dr. Hamer investigated not only the symptoms that appeared in the body, but also the emotional, psychological events that occurred prior to disease appearing in the body. This work is very well documented in a book titled *Scientific Chart of Germanic New Medicine*. The book is a medical map that directly links unresolved emotional conflict events to physical disease in specific organs of the body. Dr. Hamer calls these unresolved conflicts 'conflict shock'.

Why does he call it conflict shock?

He uses the term conflict shock to describe a highly acute emotional event that catches us off guard and is a very personal incident conditioned by our past experiences, our vulnerabilities, our values and beliefs. What he has studied and proven with thousands of patients is in part what I have been sharing with you today. The invisible part of ourselves first gets hurt, our state of mind moves into conflict. In our resistance to feeling this, we avoid it. As a result, the emotional conflict remains unresolved, and eventually the invisible hurt becomes physical in the form of disease.

Dr. Hamer says that conflict shock affects us simultaneously on three levels: the mind (psyche), the brain and the organ. He says there is a direct correlation between the emotional conflict event and the conflict mass, the physical disease that shows up in the body down the track. In summary, his work shows that unresolved emotional conflict is what leads to a physical conflict mass, such as cancer and other illnesses.

Conflict resolution is very important in our healing. Dr. Hamer says that healing on a physical level only begins after the conflict is resolved. The resolution of our emotional conflicts happens within us at the level of mind, not as a result of the surgeon's knife. We don't need to wait to get cancer to start to resolve our inner conflicts. If we can be aware of any inner disturbances in our day-to-day life as they happen, we can keep ourselves in balance and avoid disease all together. The solution is what I have been sharing, Presence and Love is the key.

I agree with Dr Hamer's conclusions. Healing doesn't just happen at the level of the body, it happens at the levels of the mind, the brain and the organs of the body. The process of physical healing only begins as we resolve our inner conflict. This process is from the inside out.

What does Dr Hamer say about the use of Chemotherapy?

His take on cancer and chemotherapy is quite interesting. With regards to cancer he says that nothing is malignant in nature and through his life's work, he concludes that the symptoms of cancer are part of the process of the body healing itself and that chemotherapy interrupts the natural healing process.

As I shared earlier, it is important to tune in and see what is right for you. What is right for one person may not be right for another. If you sense chemotherapy is right for you, then use it. If you feel it is not right for you, listen to and follow that inner guidance.

I'm just so afraid that none of this is in my control, because my mother and her mother died of cancer around the same age I am right now. What about the genes I inherited, doesn't that control my destiny?

This is a common misunderstanding that we are victims of heredity, destined to an outcome according to the genes we inherit.

In some ways we can follow our parents footsteps in the area of disease, but it is not because of our genes, it is because of our mind and our level of consciousness that can be just like our parents. After we are born it's our parents who raise us, shape us and show us how to be. In most cases we follow the same footsteps in regards to consciousness or unconsciousness as our parents, and in this way we can follow their ways to ill health, but only if we remain asleep at the wheel.

Asleep at the wheel?

In the first seven years, we are like giant sponges, and we record everything our parents tell us in the subconscious part of our mind. In short, our mind gets programmed, we inherit the ways of our parents. Of course our parents mean us no harm, but you must remember, their gods were their parents, and so the same teachings, the same beliefs, ideals, the same patterns are adopted in generation after generation within families, until someone in the hereditary chain becomes consciously aware. Then a shift happens and the pattern dissolves and is not passed down to the next generation in the family.

So if we remain unconscious, 'asleep at the wheel', our mind will work much the same way as our parents did, and we will likely respond to life's events the same way they did because our level of conscious awareness, our point of view will be very similar to theirs. It is our lack of awareness that causes us to repeat the patterns of our parents, including the patterns that lead to ill health.

However, as soon as we become aware, everything changes. As we start living with awareness we no longer react to life's events automatically, from patterns we adopted from others. You can literally 'change your mind' with regards to disease and the signals that activate genes. When we 'change our mind', we affect our genes and DNA directly.

But my parents were really nice, I love them!

I have nothing against your parents, my parents or anyone's parents. We are simply a product of our upbringing. So what this means is that we usually take on the traits, the beliefs, the ideals, the thought processes, and even create a similar bank of stories as our parents.

Following what I have been sharing with you today, it is the mind, our psyche that matters – the body and the genes follow the mind and its workings. When it comes to our genes, what is most important is the environment that your genes live in.

Environment?

The environment I am talking about is consciousness, the level of awareness, or the lack of awareness that you live with day-to-day. This consciousness is the ever important environment that your genes, your cells and your very self lives and breathes in.

We are made up of trillions of cells, this is your gene pool. Any gene that is inherently pre-disposed to disease still requires a signal for the gene to be activated. So your environment of consciousness or the lack of consciousness is a very important consideration for gene health. *Disharmony in all its forms can only happen in unconsciousness.*

But hasn't science proven that the genes we inherit can lead to disease?

Have you heard about the cell biologist Dr. Bruce Lipton?

No.

Bruce H. Lipton, PhD is a leading cell biologist, research scientist, author and former medical school teacher. He is highly sought after throughout the world as a result of his ground-breaking research showing genes and DNA do not control our biological destiny. His findings are detailed in his bestselling book titled *The Biology of Belief: Unleashing the Power of Consciousness, Matter & Miracles.* His research shows that our DNA is controlled by signals from *outside* the cell, including the energetic messages emanating from our positive or negative thoughts, in other words, our mind. What he concludes is that we are not victims of our DNA or our heredity.

Signals outside the cell?

He is talking about the environment we live in, and this environment is our state of consciousness. Are we living unconsciously, aligned with negative repetitive thoughts and actions or are we living consciously, aware of what is happening in the moment? In an environment without awareness, we are at the destiny of the patterns we have already adopted by our parents and our heritage. In an environment of conscious awareness, we write our own destiny. The environment decides the outcome of the genes and their activation. The moment we wake up and bring awareness to the equation, we can break the loop in the hereditary chain.

What was his name again? Bruce ...?

Dr. Bruce Lipton. I was lucky to have seen Bruce speak on two occasions in Australia. In those talks he said it is the environment that matters when it comes to your genes and DNA. Let me try to explain it with an example. Say there are two babies, identical twin boys that get adopted out at birth to two different families. Baby 1 goes to a home that is extremely dysfunctional and baby 2 goes to a home that is stable, supportive and loving. The environment, and the level of consciousness being experienced in day-to-day life is completely different for each boy, yet at birth their gene pool was identical. As they go through life, this background environment will shape their state of mind, attitude and point of view that comes to life in their experiences. As the two environments are so vastly different, the realised level of consciousness within each boy becomes vastly different. As a result a gene pool pre-disposed to disease could get activated in one boy and not the other.

Consciousness is the environment. Lower consciousness is linked with negative life draining energies, and higher consciousness is linked with positive life giving forces. The state of your genes, the signals that are sent to the genes to activate something, happens as a result of your inner state. So if you find yourself with a belief that you are pre-disposed to disease, or if you find yourself already in a life threatening situation like cancer, you can literally 'change your mind' about it and cure it!

Come on, change your mind to cure cancer?

This is how Dr. Bruce Lipton himself put it. In his presentation in Australia, Bruce talked about how we are not victims to our hereditary genes or DNA, and he spoke specifically about cancer and so called incurable cancer, saying ***"If you change your mind, incurables can be cured instantly".***

I happened to meet him and his wife early in the morning on the last day of this conference. I had arrived early and was outside standing in line for coffee and turned around and they were right behind me. I introduced myself and thanked him for his presentation the previous day. I told him that I am one of the people he was talking about in his presentation when he said "People with incurable cancer can cure it by 'Changing Their Mind'. He was very interested to hear my story and asked me to share what happened. I gave him a quick rundown, how I had an advanced stage of cancer in 1999, and then after the operation I woke in the most physical pain of my life but for some reason I was in gratitude for everything. I explained how my cells spoke to me, telling me to search for the cause of the cancer. And that within a month, I uncovered the emotional cause behind the cancer, and in seeing what was true, the false dissolved. As the false disappeared, what remained was a new perspective. A new point of view based on truth. In short, I had 'changed my mind' about cancer, and it was cured.

What did they think of your story?

They were delighted to hear my story. Bruce enthusiastically encouraged me to share my story with the world. He explained that my story is important because lots of people are talking about this stuff, but I have lived it, and that makes all the difference in the world to those looking for answers. Bruce suggested I write and talk about what happened, to share how I changed my mind, because through my experience, people would see the truth of it. He is a big reason why I am talking to you today.

But what exactly does he mean by 'change your mind'?

Well, 'change your mind' is something we do all the time. For example, say your husband wants to take you to see a specific movie. You read a review of the movie, and you come to think that the movie is no good. Although you don't want to see the movie, you go and see it anyway. You watch the movie and it turns out to be a very compelling story that really touches you. You change your mind and now think that the movie is wonderful. What is changing your mind? The mind is a bundle of thoughts, so 'changing your mind' is really just to change your thought about something. And 'changing your mind' can also be done with disease, because what lies behind disease is a bundle of thoughts, stories and beliefs that become entwined with our sense of self that we hold onto. Like the movie you saw with your husband, you have to be willing to become still for a little while and 'watch' the screen of your self to change your mind.

Cancer got me curious, and I started looking through new eyes. The eyes of awareness are like the eyes of an innocent child. By looking inward through these eyes, I saw the truth from the falseness, and 'changed my mind' regarding my cancer. With this change of mind my thoughts changed, my story changed, a new point of view was born, and the energetic hurt behind the cancer went flat like a dead battery. To put it in Bruce's words: The 'incurable' was cured in that instant.

Lily, we are free to 'change our mind' about any situation we face and we are free to 'change our mind' about any story, belief or thought we cling to. As you 'change your mind' in this moment, you literally choose a different future, as the next moment is born from this moment. *By looking at the hidden thoughts behind life situations with the eyes of awareness, a new future is born.*

~ 22 ~

The purpose of life is Living

Steven, are you a spiritual person? Is what you are teaching me some form of religion or spirituality?

Well it depends on what you consider spirituality to be. People have all sorts of ideas of what this is. My definition of spirituality is simply *the discovery of the self*. In the discovery of the self, you first discover what you are not, and then the true self is seen. I was watching TV last night, a show with the Australian actor and comedian Shaun Micallef. He did a series where he went to India in search of his own spirituality. While there he met a great Indian master, a guru who elegantly explained what spirituality is. He said *spirituality is a process of de-identification and re-identification*. In a way, cancer and spirituality have a lot in common. They can both bring us to a focus where we start to investigate the question, Who Am I? Being present with that question we first discover who we aren't, and then we realise the truth.

Looking at my cancer healing experience, it is really a discovery of the truth, nothing more. We see what is false, and then discover the truth and healing happens spontaneously. *Spirituality is simply the uncovering of the truth of our selves and our reality. On this road we encounter what is false and let it go. As we let go of what is false, we become more realised.*

More realised?

Yes, our consciousness shifts upwards as the false dissolves and we realise more of who we are. It is simply a self-discovery, the realisation of what we already are and have always been.

Yet, there are no goals in spirituality, as we move past resistance and start to investigate the truth, the shift happens naturally. It is not a 'doing' or a 'becoming', it is a 'realising', an 'unfolding', because you are already all the things associated with the highest levels of consciousness but you don't know it yet.

I recall someone asking Rahasya "What is the purpose of Life?" and he said **the purpose of life is 'Living', and to perhaps leave the planet a little better than we found it when we go.**[R] There is such a beautiful simplicity in his answer. He didn't say that the purpose of life is 'becoming' or 'achieving' or 'getting', it is simply 'living'. There are no goals in this purpose. We are simply here to live fully, to be our self, to experience this thing called life in all its shades and colours. *Resisting what life brings is the opposite of our purpose, no wonder so many of us fall out of balance and become sick.*

In our habitual avoidance of outer situations and inner feelings, we avoid life instead of live it. It's no coincidence that so many people who have had a challenging illness such as cancer, look back at their experience and call it a blessing.

Why would anyone call cancer a blessing?

This is because when cancer comes they become present, and life happens only in the present moment. They start to investigate and question things about their life and how they have been living. They start to discover who they really are and become real. They let go of who they are not and the false things they have been chasing. They start enjoying the moment instead of postponing life to some future time and place when their preconceived conditions are met. In short, they start living.

> Steven, how do I deal with the people around me? Now that I have cancer, my friends are suddenly acting really weird around me. They don't joke with me anymore, they treat me like a big apology, like I am a frail victim. They seem so uncomfortable around me now and many don't like coming around anymore. When they do come to see me, I feel like I have to act like a 'cancer person' just to put them at ease. If I joke around with them, they look at me like I am crazy, like I am in denial. The truth is, I feel fine most of the time, yet other times I just cry and cry. In the moments I feel fine, I don't want to have to act like a 'cancer person'. How do I deal with my friends treating me this way?

Lily, friends and family are likely finding your situation very confronting. It requires them to look at things that they may have never looked at before, and the reality of the situation can bring up a lot of fear and worry. As they look at you, they are subconsciously confronted with the fragility of their own life. In our society, we are not taught about death and dying, so we rarely look at it. When it's suddenly in front of us, reflected in the face of our best friend who has cancer, many people become uncomfortable and react with resistance in some way wanting to avoid the reality that confronts them. So what to do? Really, ***all you can do is be yourself.*** [R]

The situation is curious, as soon as someone is diagnosed with cancer, they get labelled. You are no longer John Smith or Sally Frank, you are 'cancer'. So it is a great sign that you are asking this question, which shows that you have not taken on the label of cancer as a new identity. You just want to be you, and you want your friends to just treat you 'as you' and not as 'cancer' or a victim. So just be yourself. What else can you ever be but yourself? ***The universe celebrates when you are yourself*** .[R]

You are not cancer or a victim unless you believe yourself to be. The identities we take on are just a series of thoughts. Some people in your situation take on the identity of a victim, knowingly or unknowingly using that to get something from others in return, whatever the motive. With presence, you stay clear of victim consciousness, take responsibility, experience the situation that is here. This is what I call living, our purpose for being here. ***Being yourself is the best medicine for everything in this life.***[R]

~ *23* ~

Vibration, Consciousness and your State of Health

Steven, how do you know all this stuff?

I came to know it through experiencing it and by having an incredible teacher who appeared just at the right moment to guide me. Most of what I am sharing with you today is a result of him. He pointed me to discovering these things through his teachings and my experiencing.

Dr. Kraft?

Yes, Rahasya. There is an old saying: '*When the student is ready the teacher appears*', and this is what happened with me. I was willing to do whatever it took to survive and uncover the cause of the cancer I was facing. I was so lucky to find him, or should I say I was lucky he found me.

He found you?

In India they say, the Guru chooses the disciple.

Guru?

Guru simply means teacher, it typically refers to a teacher who is realised at a high level of consciousness.

He chose you?

That's what I feel happened at the end of my second meeting with Rahasya at Mevlana. He invited me to join the counselling for counsellors course. Whichever way I look at how we came together, it was perfect, meant to be, the universe conspiring to bring balance.

Did you stay in contact with Rahasya after Mevlana?

After my time at Mevlana, I lost touch with Rahasya for a period of ten years. I lived eight hours away in Sydney and Rahasya was teaching all around the world for most of each year. In Sydney I went back to running my software company, but after returning to work I found that my heart was no longer in running that company.

Inside I felt a calling to go in another direction. This calling was encouraging me to let my company go, and to write a book about what happened at Mevlana to share what Rahasya showed me which led to the spontaneous healing of my cancer.

I am a talented software designer, a master builder of computer business systems, but my heart called out to go in another direction.

No longer controlled by the mind and 'becoming,' I could now follow my heart and move away from business and share what I learned, to help people help themselves as I had helped myself. A book about this experience, sharing what I learned as a result of Rahasya and his teachings was a good place to start.

I know how focused and driven you were in business. Was it hard to let your software company go?

Yes, it took me over 8 years to let it go. This calling to write a book came soon after Mevlana, yet I had a acute addiction to achieving and becoming successful, so to let go of the company I gave birth to, was extremely hard to do. As I moved to sell my company, I came close to the edge of selling it a number of times, but stepped back out of fear of what it meant for me and my family's future, and an inner resistance that didn't want to let go of the 'successful business man' tag I had strived to create for myself. My business and being a success in business was a big part of who I thought I was at the time. Finally, in May of 2009, after many aborted attempts, I let it go, sold the company to the other directors and walked away. For the first time in 18 years, I had open space to just be and explore my heart's desire. I began writing the book *Inner Sky*, and as soon as I started writing an amazing synchronicity happened that reunited me with Rahasya ten years after I had first meet him at Mevlana.

Synchronicity?

You know, something that happens and you realise that it couldn't be by chance – a coincidence that can't be coincidental. It is when something bigger than you has it's hands on the wheel of your life and things start happening, the stars align and bring you exactly what you need at that very moment.

I had been writing for some weeks when I came to write about the fifth day of the course at Mevlana. Rahasya came rushing into my thoughts and I wondered where he was as I hadn't seen him in ten years. I wrote a note to myself on a piece of paper "Find Rahasya and ask him what really happened on the fifth day of the course." I needed some practical answers for the book to bridge the gap between the science and spirituality.

The very next day Angelina's car was booked to go into the mechanics. I met her at a local café for a coffee before she was to follow me to drop off her car. After the coffee, I went out to my car which was parked tightly between two other cars. I opened my door and squeezed into the drivers seat. As I went to close my door, two people walked between my car and the adjacent car, trying to get past but blocked by my open door that I was trying to pull shut. I looked up and it was none other than Rahasya and his wife Nura!

No way ... Incredible!

I jumped out of the car, "Rahasya!" He greeted me with a huge smile and a big hug. He asked what I was doing here in the far north coast, and I shared that I now lived nearby. I told him that I had been thinking about him the day before because I am writing a book about resistance and my spontaneous healing, and had some questions about what happened at Mevlana.

Rahasya said he was in Byron Bay for a few more days before he went overseas to run courses in Europe and Asia, so we arranged a meeting at his house where I could interview him to get the answers.

So what happened when you saw him? What did he tell you?

Well, I had a few days to prepare my questions. I was looking to understand the link between the inner experience I had to the physical outcome where cancer was cured. I was looking for answers hoping to create a bridge of understanding for the book.

When I arrived, Rahasya greeted me in his driveway. The first thing I noticed was that he looked exactly the same as he did ten years ago. His face and body had not aged one bit.

We walked down a stone path through a magnificent garden of tropical plants surrounded in giant bamboo to a wooden Japanese looking building near the back of his property. We stepped into his studio nestled in gardens next to a pool. The room was warmly decorated and the sunlight streamed in through the windows onto the two seats facing each other in the middle of the floor. I was nervous, not having seen him for so long, but I settled as Rahasya started the session with some simple conversation and a short meditation.

I explained to him that I wanted to share my healing experience with others so they could learn and benefit from it. To achieve this I hoped to understand things from three interlinking perspectives: Spiritual, Emotional and Physical (scientific). I shared with Rahasya that with his expertise as a medical doctor and his mastery in the spiritual, mental and emotional areas, I hoped he could help me bridge this gap.

I had prepared twenty questions. After a brief refresher on my life in the years since I saw him, the interview started.

What did you ask him?

I was mainly curious about the science behind how resistance to emotional experiences leads to sickness. I asked him how our repressed emotions affect the cells of our body, and how repressed emotions get stuck at the cellular level within the body?

And ...

Rahasya explained resistance in terms of vibration. He said that to understand how resistance affects us, we need to think of ourselves as more than just a solid form, because behind our solid appearance, we are made up of cells. He explained that cells are vibration. From a simplified scientific perspective, our physical bodies are made up of trillions of cells. These cells are made up of molecules that are simply groups of atoms bound together. Atoms are the building blocks of everything in the universe. Anything physical is made of atoms. So to answer my question he said it was important to view things from the perspective of atoms and cells, the vibrational stuff we are made of.

If you were to look deep within an atom with a super-powered microscope, there wouldn't be much to see, because 99.9% of the volume that comprises an atom is 'empty space.' In other words, you, me, my dog and that tree over there are 99.9% space.

Then why are we solid?

It is the vibrational properties of the atom that creates this effect.

Our eyes see the human body as solid and physical, because the elements within the trillion of cells that make up our bodies are constantly spinning and vibrating. It is the atoms' vibration, the orbital spinning of the elements within the atoms of our cells that gives us the appearance of a solid body. Rahasya explained that *we are simply the effects of the vibration of our cells.*[R]

Why is this important?

Rahasya said it's important that we look behind this 'solid' appearance and understand that we are fundamentally vibrational beings and our vibration is extremely important in regards to our state of health and wellbeing.

Rahasya reminded me of the term 'Pain Body' in this interview, explaining it as the accumulated emotional pain not fully faced or accepted in the moment it arose. He linked our discussion of vibration to the Pain Body in saying that the Pain Body itself is energetic in nature and vibrational in form, meaning it is first invisible to the human eye but can eventually solidify and become visible where it is diagnosed as a disease.

Rahasya said that *vibration has a direct affect on vibration.* [R] We get sick because the vibration of the Pain Body takes up residency within the organs of our body. The Pain Body being an energetic vibrational disturbance, directly and vibrationally affects the cells in and around the organs it resides within. This negatively impacts your state of health at the level of mind and body. In other words, before the physical body gets sick, the psyche gets sick, the energy of the person gets disturbed, which perpetuates to physical disease in unconsciousness, our resistance to experience.

This correlates completely with my experience at Mevlana. I had repressed anger since childhood, a Pain Body held in the organs of my lower belly, the seat of emotions. In my ongoing resistance to experiencing this anger, I unknowingly kept the Pain Body alive and fuelled it. The energetic vibrational Pain Body of anger sitting in my lower belly was a vibrational disturbance that had a harmful affect on the cells of the organs in my lower belly and bowel. This invisible negative vibrational disturbance directly affected the cells of my bowel until one more acute and painful incident related to the same core hurt, became the final straw where the invisible vibrational disturbance that I have been calling the Pain Body, became visible and was labelled Bowel cancer.

How does this come about, why do we resist?

We resist for a lot of different reasons, but one of the main reasons we resist is our attachment to who we think we are, the sense of self we derive from our Pain Body. Disease can be born from our Pain Body, yet it is quite common that we unknowingly hold onto our Pain Body, feed it and fight to protect it.

That's crazy, why would we want to protect our pain?

Rahasya explained that we unknowingly form a bond with our Pain Body, we become attached to our unresolved hurt's vibrational pattern. That pattern becomes us because we derive a sense of self from it. Think about what happened with me. Behind my Pain Body was the false 'story of me', a story I told myself throughout my life. A story of victimhood and abandonment, filled with feelings, emotions and memories that I believed to be true. As I believed this 'story of me' I became it, derived a sense of self from it, and therefore perpetuated it throughout my life.

I held onto the Pain Body by resisting it. I feed the Pain Body with each new hurtful experience that I buried under my skin. Who

I thought I was was linked to this vibrational pattern. And of course we will do just about anything to protect the 'me' we come to see. So we unknowingly protect the Pain Body that we vibrate with and have become.

And so it goes, the story of resistance, we will do whatever it takes to avoid what we don't want, and to hold onto our definition of self. As we keep our eyes shut and remain unaware, the Pain Body perpetuates, and we unknowingly support it through our resistance to it.

As a result, we have a situation where subconsciously we don't want to get rid of the Pain Body because to get rid of it, is to get rid of the very thing we have come to know ourselves to be. This brings us back to one of the biggest challenges of cancer and other illness. People stop at the door to looking at what's behind their illness because if they resolve the cause, then it is a kind of death of them, a death of what they have come to know themselves to be. What I call the death without dying.

Death without dying?

Yes, the death of the false you, the Ego and the attachments to stories, beliefs and experiences from the past that we cling to and define ourselves by. Our biggest addiction is our identity. So we get stuck and have a resistance to even considering looking at the things we derive a 'self' from, because to see the truth behind the stories of our mind, means our very 'self' is at risk of being annihilated.

Living unconsciously in this way, many people would rather deal with cancer in an outward physical way with operation after operation, than look inwards and risk the death of their defined 'self.' So they stay in resistance and look everywhere else for a solution, never stepping up to the plate to take a swing at the truth. This is resistance in action, one of the biggest hurdles to resolving cancer and other forms of disease.

How did you manage to get past this resistance?

For me, the risk of physical death was enough for me to stop running and take a swing. Cancer was a doorway to the truth of me. Yes there was a death without dying, a death of the false 'me', that part of me that considered itself to be abandoned and a victim. With this death of the false, everything I had been clinging to behind the old 'story of me' vanished into thin air.

We don't die?

When we lose what we falsely believe ourselves to be, we don't die, because the false self is really just an absence, it never existed in the first place. Cancer silently asks 'Do you have the courage to let everything you know yourself to be die, and in doing so be born fresh and begin to live?'

Were you afraid?

Yes, but in the face of physical death, I became present enough to accept the reality of the situation. Courage came as an element of this presence, which allowed me to accept the death of everything I falsely thought I was.

I 'm afraid too!

Lily, it's not you that's afraid, it's the conditioned mind that resists change. The mind just needs to relax a little bit, like what happened to me when I was in the shower three days after my diagnosis, and what happened when I was sitting on the couch with Rahasya on the morning of the fifth day of the counselling course at Mevlana. Remember what Rahasya said to me? "Steven this is a wonderful news! You are not losing your mind, the anxiety is just the mind trying to let things up slowly, you can relax, it's natural, this is nature's way." With his words, my mind relaxed and let it happen. My walls of resistance came down and dared to experience what was at the core of me. In allowing, I experienced what I had been resisting, the false me departed, the true me was exposed and the cause of cancer was healed instantly.

You are not your mind, so don't let it get in your way. Through presence you will befriend the mind, and it will serve you like a faithful knight serves his queen.

In the interview did Rahasya explain why the healing happened?

He said that the solution has to do with consciousness, because when we are present and bring awareness within, this is how we become one with whatever we are resisting. As we become one with whatever we are resisting, it dissolves. Another way to say this is that through awareness, consciousness rises and the Pain Body simply dissolves.

So the Pain Body actually dissolves?

The Pain Body can only exist as we remain unaware and resistant.

With awareness the Pain Body can not perpetuate.

Rahasya said vibration affects vibration. As we live with awareness, our consciousness rises. As consciousness rises, our vibration rises and the Pain Body which is a lower vibration cannot co-exist with the vibration of your higher consciousness.

The higher vibration cancels the Pain Body?

The Pain Body which encompasses our unresolved emotional hurts is unconscious, a low vibration energetic entity. Conscious awareness is a highly conscious vibrational entity. As these two vibrations meet, as in the fifth day of my counselling course at Mevlana, the higher vibration of consciousness (truth) cancels out the lower vibration of the Pain Body (what is false).

Awareness is a higher energy than thought.[R] What's behind the Pain Body is just thoughts, and false stories that we believe to be true, yet refuse to look at openly. If the two meet, what remains is the higher vibration of awareness, the truth.

Bruce Lipton explains this vibrational cancelling effect very well in his book *The Biology of Belief*. In summary, the higher vibration waves of awareness neutralise the lower vibration waves of the Pain Body in much the same way as two waves coming together on a pond from opposite directions have a cancelling effect. When two waves on a body of water hit each other, the more powerful wave neutralises (cancels out) the smaller wave. This is a scientifically proven rule that correlates to our vibrational state of health.

When truth meets what is false, the same thing happens. The Pain Body is just a dark room, a room absent of light. Awareness is the light source. When awareness enters a dark room the darkness dissolves, because the darkness is just an absence of light: what is false dissolves in truth, because what is false is just the absence of truth.

The Pain Body is never the truth, it is created and can only exist in our unconsciousness. As the Pain Body is met with conscious awareness, the story of suffering is over.

Let me draw you a simple equation I came up with to explain it, I call it the *Consciousness Equation.*

Consciousness = Perception = Vibration = State of Health

A change to any part of this equation changes all other components, as they are directly related in every way. An upward shift in your consciousness will have a radical change in how you experience your reality (perception). The vibration of your cells will increase, you will feel lighter, more energetic, and your state of health will improve. You can approach the equation from the middle or the end. For example, a shift in your perception shifts your consciousness, increases your vibration and brings health. As the equation shows, each component can be substituted for another as they are literally one the same.

With regards to vibration and our health, Rahasya reminded me why he stopped practicing as a medical doctor. The medical doctor is at the end of the line, dealing with the physical body after illness appears. He sees that before the physical body gets sick, the psyche gets sick, illness begins in our energy field, when our vibration gets disturbed.

The cells of the body just follow what they are given.[R] So if there is a long held inner conflict, the cells of the body simply follow the environment they live in. In my case, cancer was the result. The opposite is also true. Bring awareness to your environment, and the cells of the body follow what they are given, with spontaneous healing often the result.

Tying it all together, Rahasya shared the secret to spontaneous healing. He said that I had a shift in consciousness, where I discovered a new sense of me that no longer resisted my inner experience. In this state of openness, I allowed myself to experience what I had avoided for 30 years and became one with it. In experiencing the repressed anger, awareness was brought to what had been unconscious within. The higher vibration of awareness dissolved the lower vibration of the unconscious Pain Body and the cells of my body simply followed what they were given.

Rahasya concluded our interview by saying: ***This is how spontaneous healing of anything happens. You lift the level of consciousness and everything happens.***[R]

~ 24 ~

Whatever you become
one with turns to joy

Steven, you have mentioned the word 'energy' a few times, can you explain what you mean by this?

Let me try and explain it to you through the work of the world's most famous scientist, Albert Einstein. His great work was all about energy. His famous equation $E=mc^2$, is the Mass-Energy equivalence. I just call it the equation of Energy. In short, this equation says that Energy (E) and Matter (M) are one and the same, that anything that has a Mass has an equivalent amount of Energy and anything that has Energy has an equivalent amount of Mass.

Matter?

Matter is anything that is physical, occupies space and has a mass. Like you, me, this kitchen table, and that tree over there. Einstein says that Energy is Matter, and Matter is Energy. The two words are interchangeable. *Energy is the invisible form of something and Matter is it's physical form.*

They are the same?

Yes, two states of their same-self. In some circumstances a thing is visible and has mass. In other circumstances a thing is invisible and has no detectable mass that our eyes can see. This invisible energetic form of something is what I have been referring to as energy. Einstein proved that Matter and Energy are not two different things, they are two sides of the same coin. So what I bring to your attention is that what a doctor calls cancer, which is a visible mass of cells within the body, is also energy. *Everything in this universe that we see and don't see is comprised of energy.*

It's just how you look at things. Like distance between two locations, you can talk about the distance as miles or kilometres, but they are both talking about the same thing, distance. Literally Matter and Energy are interchangeable.

So how does this relate to me?

The Pain Body is an invisible energetic form of pain, an Energy that doesn't have a mass we can see. *What's behind the Pain Body are our thoughts, that come together in our stories, that become concrete in our beliefs, that we become attached to as our sense of self, that at a certain threshold turn into Matter, our physical biology called our body.*

Thoughts are the building blocks of our inner pain. And thoughts are nothing more then energy, an invisible energetic entity.

How are thoughts energy?

Thoughts are measurable, they have a frequency, the vibration of their waves can be measured. Thought energy travels outwards from their source, much like a wave on the ocean.

So behind the Pain Body are energetic thoughts that accumulate in our stories, beliefs, and feelings, forming an energetic entity whose vibrations travel outwards from where the Pain Body is stored within the organs of the body. As energy we can sometimes feel it, some inner disturbance for example, but we cannot see it in physical form until the accumulation of energy reaches a threshold where it becomes a visible form of its same-self that can then be labelled as something like cancer or some other disease of the body.

Does Einstein's equation show how to reverse the cell growth once it has appeared?

Let me give you a simple analogy of energy as a moving car. Say you are driving and your foot is on the accelerator and the car is travelling at a velocity of 200 miles per hour. How do you stop the car? Take your foot off the accelerator and the velocity will slow and the car will come to a stop. It is the same with the energetic energy behind our Pain Body. Through awareness we eliminate the source of fuel for our Pain Body, neutralising it and bringing the energy of the Pain Body to a stop. *Where there is no velocity, there is no energy and no mass.* Like the moving car, the Pain Body must come to a stop when it runs out of fuel. As in my case on the fifth day of the counselling course there was no longer any velocity behind the Pain Body and as a result there was no way to even start that vehicle called cancer anymore.

The equation points the way. As Matter and Energy are two

states of the same-self, if you take away the energy behind the physical Matter by neutralising it, then the physical mass which no longer has energy, is also neutralised. Or as Rahasya so nicely put it, *the cells of the body just follow what they are given*. The physical body is a little slower to respond, but when the energy within the cells shifts, the body follows.

OK, so with regards to our health and healing, our thoughts matter!

Yes, and awareness is the key to shifting our view of things, to altering the velocity of our thoughts about something, to 'change our mind' and bring things back into harmony.

Lily, awareness is the key, and one of the first things we should become aware of is our resistance. It's our resistance to hurts that we don't want to experience that keeps our foot pushing down on the accelerator. *The fuel for the Pain Body is resistance!* In other words, our Pain Body can only exist in our resistance to it. Stepping through the door of our resistance to meet what is here is the first step. This is how we take our foot off the accelerator.

Rahasya said the same thing in terms of vibration: fear, stress, guilt, anger, all these 'negative emotions' have a lower vibration that perpetuates itself through resisting it. It's our resistance that gives the Pain Body life in the first place and it's our resistance that sustains it. Resisting is the only way to keep the vibration low. *The moment you un-resist, the flood of life washes it clean.*[R]

I am starting to understand what you mean by resistance, but what if I find something inside I don't want!

The very fact that you are resisting, means there is a story, an interpretation of something you don't want. The act of letting go is an act of surrendering to what is here. In other words, whatever you find, just be receptive and observe it. If feelings or sensations arise, just feel it in your body. If emotions arise welcome the emotions. You don't need to 'do' anything else, you don't need to change whatever is observed. If you have a goal to change whatever you find, that is the active mind trying to control the very thing you are simply inviting to be here. The beauty is, all you need to do is stop running and become aware. Be a witness to that which you have been resisting, and the flood of life will wash it clean.

But what if I start crying and never stop?

If crying happens, then let it happen. If it happens every day non-stop for one week, two weeks, a month … let it happen. It is our wanting things to be different than What Is, which is behind our resistance. So if crying happens, then accept the crying and become one with it by welcoming and experiencing it.

Whatever you move into a state of presence with you become one with, and **whatever you become one with turns to joy.**[R] Resistance and conflict stops because you can't be against something that you're already one with. *Healing is the result when we are no longer separate from ourselves.*

Rahasya says it another way: ***The way to raise the vibration of the cells and heal is really very, very simple. You become one with the experience of this moment – that is all.*** [R]

So Lily, I say cry away if that is what comes. Just be with whatever is happening. There is nothing to fear, because the only thing you can find beneath your inner clouds is the real you, and the real you is love.

But how do I become one with things?

Through experiencing, meeting what is here right now. There are many ways, you don't need to go to Mevlana and have six days of intensive counselling course for it to happen. Each of us has our own path, and all paths lead to the top of the mountain, so follow what's right for you.

Where can I start?

You can start applying this day-to-day. If someone hurts you, you become one with the pain. Experience the pain, welcome it, observe it as a witness, feel it in the body, don't push it away or try to change what's happening. If someone brings you joy, you become one with the joy. Then you discover that all negative emotions such as fear, stress, pain, anger, disappointment, jealousy, all these so called 'negative experiences' dissolve when you become one with them because as you are one with them, the energy behind them comes and goes, and does not form clouds within your Inner Sky.

This seems like a lot of work!

It might seem that way, but as you experiment with this, you will see it becomes natural, a normal way of being. Those parts of you that are held separate can be revealed gradually, in your own time and space. As you experience whatever is here in your daily life instead of resisting, all the energy you used towards resisting is returned to you and you will find yourself more energised and life has a new bounce. What at this point might seem like 'work', turns into something that renews you and fills you with energy.

Living with awareness in day-to-day life is a very effective path you can explore, and it may be all you need without taking external courses or counselling. It depends on where you're at consciously. If you haven't meditated before, you may want to join a meditation group or find someone to help you get started. Life is a great teacher and day-to-day life will bring you experiences that give you an opportunity to meet that part of yourself that is being held separate. As you live with this awareness, you will become one with your experiences as they happen, and conflicts will resolve as they appear.

Can you give me an example of this?

OK. Say you and I are in a relationship and I do something that pushes your buttons and you feel angry. Say your normal reaction to this type of situation is to suppress your anger. To bring awareness to this day-to-day situation, you witness the anger arising within you as it happens. You move to experience the anger in the moment it arises instead of hiding your anger. So for example, a first step to experiencing the anger would be to express it so you can actually feel it. You could go into your bedroom and bang a cushion and scream at the top of your lungs. This really can be very helpful. The next step in experiencing that anger would be to observe it. While you are still in your bedroom, a quiet space where you won't be interrupted, sit quietly and explore what is here. In this space, don't push anything away, invite and relive the experience that caused you to feel angry. The body is a good place to experience, so feel it in the sensations of your body. Just be a silent witness to whatever is here. You may see things behind your eyes as you meditate, you may get a message, you may have body sensations, there is nothing you need to find and there is nothing you need to change. Each time your experience may be totally different, so try not to hold any expectations. In short, be your own scientist investigating and observing everything that's here with your experiences.

Shouldn't I get rid of the anger?

No, you don't need to get rid of anything. You don't throw the anger out, don't hold the anger down or run away from the anger. Don't get violent with the person who pushed your buttons. You don't need to change or do anything to the experience, just observe, investigate and feel it.

But what if I am out shopping or what if I am at work when someone pushes my buttons? I can't express anger in front of all my employees!

In those situations where you become aware of anger while you're in public or at work, you can delay your response. Maybe you have to wait until you get home or you find an unused meeting room. As soon as possible, find a quiet space and invite that experience back and relive it. As you become one with the experience, it moves through you and completes. Become one with anger and immediately the anger will guide you into what it's covering up. Beneath anger we may discover hurt and pain, then we move to experience pain and uncover what is underneath that. What we eventually find under any hurt or pain as we become one with it is space, which is another way of saying joy and love, the real you, the true self.

When you live this way, what you'll find is that you don't need hours of therapy with a psychologist. You just need a minute of being fully present with what is here. Rahasya explains it succinctly this way: ***You experience what is here in its totality and you become one with it, and very quickly it opens you to Love, because that is who you are.*** [R]

~ 25 ~

Who are you without the story?

Thank you Steven, I will try this. Any other suggestions that might help me immediately deal with this situation?

There are some common approaches to healing that work. But I think what you're asking me is, are there other approaches besides something like counselling or therapy to achieve the same result?

Yes, that is what I want to know.

There are many ways, but let me share one approach that comes to mind from my own recent experiences.

There is a direct approach where we go straight to the heart of the situation and bypass the stories of the mind to see the truth that lies past our stories. This is very direct route, this approach can be appropriate for some people and not for others.

OK, what is it?

Rahasya has been teaching and helping people heal themselves for over 33 years. I was in a course in Dalian, China with Rahasya recently, and noticed a distinct change of approach and I felt his teaching went to a new level. In this course, Rahasya was going directly to the heart with people, with less processing and analysis of each person's story. He was directly leading people right past their story to discover the truth behind the story.

What was he doing?

Each day in the course there were a few hours of one-on-one sessions with Rahasya called Satsang. Satsang is an ancient word meaning 'meeting in truth', or simply 'being with the truth'. What happens in Satsang is that Rahasya sits in the front of the room and there is a special chair for someone to sit with him, to sit in their truth completely. Satsang is very similar to what happened on the morning of the fifth day of my counselling course, when Rahasya invited me up to sit with him on the couch. I shared that I was feeling extremely anxious and he helped me investigate and understand what was really happening. Through our interaction, he guided me into the truth of the situation, that I was not losing my mind and the anxiety was part of the natural process.

Yes, I understand

OK, so what typically happens with Satsang is that Rahasya first runs a guided meditation to create the space for Satsang, and then after the meditation he starts the Satsang session. He starts the session by saying something like: "Welcome to Satsang … any discoveries, any inquiries, any questions, any awakenings, any sharings? You are most welcome to come sit with me."

It's typical during these courses, that many people want to sit in Satsang with Rahasya, because people are often stuck in some area in their life and don't know what to do. Often they have a challenging situation, and are looking for guidance to resolve the situation. Rahasya is also sitting in truth, and as he is realised at a high level of consciousness, the guidance and answers come through him effortlessly from the space of consciousness itself. In most cases, whatever conflict is brought to the seat of Satsang with Rahasya is resolved on the spot, through a meeting with the truth. *Consciousness has a way to bring understanding and truth into view.*

For years I watched how consciousness flows through Rahasya to guide people through their issues in a kind of therapeutic approach. Rahasya would lead each person in an investigation of the story to discover the truth behind it. It is a very effective approach, but it does take some time to explore all of the key parts of the story we tell ourselves. However, in Dalian, China I noticed he was taking a different approach in Satsang. In hearing someone's story, Rahasya would guide them a little bit, and then he would ask them to close their eyes to investigate. After guiding them inwards, Rahasya would encapsulate the story, giving a brief summary of the story the person just shared, and then he would say something like: "Who are you without the story?" or "How are you without the story?"

How does this help?

He is consciously guiding the person inwards, encapsulating the story that the person has shared, and asking them to put the story aside, to remove the story for just a minute or two. He then asks the person 'Who are you without the story'. This is a direct way to investigate the truth without the story, past the layers of the mind that can get in the way. You could say it is a kind of short cut to the truth and healing.

Does it work?

Yes. I watched the immediate shift in student after student who sat in Satsang in Dalian, and in many other courses since. At a certain level of conscious awareness a quickening happens, this approach can brings us quickly to the discovery of truth and healing, where the higher vibration of consciousness meets and dissolves the lower vibration of what had been unconscious.

This is done in front of everyone in a course?

Yes. I know that sounds confronting, but there is nothing confronting about the truth when you meet it. It is resistance, the avoidance of truth that causes us to feel uncomfortable and confronted.

As we sit with awareness in truth, what we find is that without our story we are perfectly fine.

Why did Rahasya suddenly change his approach?

After class on the third day in Dalian, I went to Rahasya's hotel to pick up a box of tea, a gift he was given that he wanted me to carry back to Australia for him as he continued travelling and teaching across Asia. Over dinner I shared my observation that I felt his teachings had gone to a new level, and that the new approach was very direct.

I asked Rahasya why he was using this new approach. He said that ever since his beloved wife Nura left her body earlier that year, his teachings had changed and had become more direct. He didn't know why, it simply was what was happening since Nura left her body.

His wife died?

Rahasya was married to an incredible enlightened German woman named Nura, whom he had met in India. They taught together throughout the world, side by side for over 30 years. The way they taught together was beautiful. It was as if they had become one person, with Rahasya bringing in the more masculine aspects in the teachings and Nura balancing the teachings from the aspect of the Divine Feminine.

In April of that year, they were teaching in Japan, and Nura suddenly became ill. A bacteria had somehow got into her brain and she abruptly fell into a coma and left her body.

He shared with me that since her passing, his teachings are more direct, with less detours. There is less processing, less time for analysing of the stories, going directly past the story to the truth. In witnessing this approach many times, I see it as a loving arrow to the heart.

Did you sit in Satsang with Rahasya?

Yes, many times. A few months after the trip to Dalian, Rahasya hosted a few nights of Satsang at his studio in Australia where I experienced this loving arrow to the heart firsthand.

Really, what happened?

In the week leading up to the Satsang night, I was having some physical problems with my body. My neck was very stiff making it hard to move my head, and my left arm was painful to move. Normally I'm in excellent physical health. My lifestyle is active, athletic and fit, and I hadn't had any physical injuries to cause these symptoms, so the situation was very strange. I just woke up one morning and couldn't lift my arm or move my neck.

In Satsang at Rahasya's studio, I sat with Rahasya to investigate what was going on. I shared a story with Rahasya about a woman I had met a few months earlier. She was the roommate of my friend Tom. The woman and I became friends and the three of us got together socially over dinner many times each week as they lived nearby. This woman was very attracted to me, and she wanted me to be her boyfriend, and she was very forthright in telling me that she wanted me "body, mind and soul". But I didn't have the same feelings for her. I just saw her as a close friend, not as a girlfriend, and I made it very clear to her that I was not interested in having an intimate relationship.

During Satsang, I shared that my friend Tom is a very aware person and he came over to my house on the morning I woke up with my neck and arm problem. He said he knows why I am having these physical problems. He said his roommate is madly in love with me, and in her mind she has painted her entire life with me. He added that she is trying to control me energetically through a psychic attack. Trying to control me so that I fall in love with her and become her boyfriend.

I believed Tom's story wholeheartedly because before Tom told me this, I had already become uncomfortable with this woman, feeling like this she was stalking me.

In the days following my talk with Tom, my neck and left arm got worse. By the time I drove to the Satsang, I couldn't lift up my left arm at all, it was like a dead weight.

In Satsang, I asked Rahasya if there is such a thing as an energetic attack?

Rahasya said: "It's interesting isn't it? Who knows what the girl is doing? What is more interesting is the story you tell yourself about this girl, that your whole sense of 'me' gets tense and feels controlled. The story is NOT about the girl, the story is about your thoughts. It's your story!"

He encapsulated my story by saying: "What is the story? The girl wants to be with you and is controlling you psychically."

Rahasya explained what was happening as a result of this story I believed. ***The Body/Mind has no idea, no discrimination between reality and a thought.***[R] To explain this he shared an analogy that when he meets with friends who talk about his late wife Nura in a very loving way, he cries. He cries even though he is very aware that it has nothing to do with the moment, it is the thought about something that happened in the past that triggers the body/mind reaction, and the body/mind thinks it's happening right now, and it's actually not true.

Rahasya then asked me to close my eyes and he guided me inwards. After a minute or so, he paused and asked: "So, who are you without this story? Who are you without this whole package?

The whole package is your friend coming to you, telling you that the woman wants to be with you and is attacking you psychically, that is your whole story. Who would you be without this whole story?"

With my eyes closed, I imagined this story not being a part of me anymore. To remove the story, I visualised putting the story in a box, and then placed the box on a shelf on the other side of the room. This felt safe because my story was in a box just over there, and I could have it back whenever I wanted. As I went inwards and investigated how I was without the story of the girl attacking me, I found that I was perfectly fine, there was no problem at all. I responded with the truth of what I was seeing and feeling. I said: "I am ... Calm ... Safe ... at Peace."

Rahasya replies: "That's right, that's the end of the story! That's the end of that sense of you, that had formed in relation to this girl. It is just a story that attaches to the Me, until you see it ... Finished!"

Rahasya explained that we can't avoid being caught by our stories. However, that is the beauty of our stories because in being caught, we can awaken to the truth. ***Our stories are a doorway and within them awareness can flower.***[R]

As the Satsang came to a close and I opened my eyes, Rahasya asked me how my neck was feeling now? I moved my neck from side to side and there was no stiffness or tension at all.

Really?

True. The physical symptoms of my neck disappeared.

What about your arm?

I didn't realise it until an hour or so later when I got in my car and started driving home. I was driving down the highway and suddenly realised I was driving with my left arm, it was normal, back to full strength.

How do you explain this?

When people see the truth beyond their story, which is just a bundle of thoughts that they are identified with, what is false is no longer, and the energy, vibration and mental effects behind the story are neutralised. Just like what happened to me on the fifth day of the course in Mevlana in 1999, another way to move beyond resistance, where life washes everything clean.

Did the pain in the neck or arm return later on?

No. That inquiry put an end to the story that my mind had made out to be real. In the days following the Satsang, no symptoms came back and I was at peace with regards to the woman. The story I had been telling myself about her was no long valid, and therefore that sense of 'me' no longer felt controlled or tense which was instantly reflected in my body.

A week after the Satsang I reflected on the instant recovery of my body. Dr. Bruce Lipton, the famous cell biologist came to mind. I remember what he said to me in Byron Bay "If you change your mind, incurables can be cured instantly." In seeing beyond our story, we get a new point of view, which is a 'change of mind'. This change is reflected in our biology, as the mind and body are interweaved as one. Rahasya and Bruce Lipton are simply using different words to communicate the same thing.

~ 26 ~

Experiencing liberates and brings us home

What did Rahasya say about your cells opening and releasing on the fifth day of the course? What was released?

I asked him what was released when I touched the suppressed anger of the Pain Body with conscious awareness.

He said what released was tension in the physical body, the suppressed psychological pain. He said that suppression takes a lot of energy to hold it in, whereas 'being' doesn't take energy, it opens to energy. So, during that counselling session, as I un-resisted, as that lid opened, all of that energy that I had been unknowingly using to hold back and suppress the emotion, was released. It was a lot of energy, a lot of mental energy and a lot of physical energy. Those energy bodies released at the same time and I experienced the physical sensation of release.

Was the Pain Body releasing?

In awakening to the truth, the false sense of self that had been part of the Pain Body was no longer, and the Pain Body dissolved. The Pain Body dissolved and all the energy I had been using to suppress and hold down the pain, suddenly released and rose up through my body. No longer in resistance, that part of me that I had denied was not held captive anymore and set free. In his explanation, Rahasya reminded me that this transpires through conscious awareness which recognises the truth. The egoic mind cannot 'do this' or go there.

And that feeling of lightness afterwards?

I asked him about this, why I felt light as a feather and why I then experienced Love in everything. He said: ***The liberation is first you release, and through the release, the core becomes more visible.***[R]

The core becomes more visible?

The authentic self, the real you; who we truly are underneath our pain bodies, the clouds that cover us up. Our core is higher consciousness, a higher octave, experienced as joy, peace and love. With the release, my consciousness shifted where my true self became more realised. I experienced this as a feeling of being set free. I felt new and alive, my body seemed physically light as a feather, and my view of things changed and suddenly I saw love in everything that was happening.

So the release liberated you?

The 'experiencing' liberated me. Becoming one with the anger, experiencing it fully as I did within the counselling session allowed the release and the liberation. **With the release the door to the core is open. It is not the release that makes the core visible, it is the experiencing.**[R]

So the key is experiencing?

Yes, you got it! *Experiencing happens in our meeting what is here, not in our contraction to what we don't want to feel.*

Awareness brought me beyond the door of resistance where I became one with anger and the release happened. 'Experiencing' enabled the true me to become visible again. *Our true nature is not something we obtain outside ourselves, it is something we already are, realised through experiencing.*

Steven, can I share something with you? I think I need to share something I never shared before.

Yes, of course.

Ummm … *[Tears well up in Lily's eyes]*

When I was sixteen years old growing up in New Zealand, I became pregnant to my first boyfriend and … *[Lily crying openly]*

It's OK, take your time.

When he found out I was pregnant, he had me come over to his mother's house.

His mother and a couple of aunties were there waiting for me. They told me I was too young to have a baby and it was best for everyone if I had an abortion. *[Lily weeps more strongly.]*

Before I knew what was happening, they had me out the back in a makeshift room and they performed the abortion themselves. It went horribly wrong and I almost died ...

I have never told anyone this story before and ...

I was so young ... It happened so fast and I didn't know what was going on ...

I never wanted to kill my baby!

I feel so guilty about losing my baby! *[Lily continues to cry]*

One month later I bought a one-way ticket to Australia and ran away from home. I only had $100 in my pocket, but I fought hard and somehow made it. I have been running from this all my life. I think about my baby every day and the pain always seeps into my life, turning days where I have every reason to be happy into sad days. *[Weeping]*

Everything you are saying rings true. I have been running away from these hurts since I was sixteen years old, and wherever I run, no matter what I do, I don't get away from the guilt and the sadness. When the doctor told me I had ovarian cancer, a picture of my boyfriend's mother and aunties flashed in my head. I see that I need to stop running away from this, and be with it now. *[Weeping]*

Thank you Steven.

I love you Lily, thank you for sharing this with me. This is a giant step towards healing.

The act of running away from New Zealand to Australia is an outer reaction of trying to escape that inner pain. We are the same, it's not by chance that I ended up in Australia too, the furthest place on the planet from America where I thought the source of my pain would stay put. It is true that whatever we resist persists. We can't run away from the hurts we resist, because we carry them with us wherever we go, until we welcome them home again.

If you can reopen the book to what happened back then and view it through the eyes of awareness, you may see things in a new light and form a new point of view. You were only 16 back then, an innocent girl turning into a woman. Life has it's own ideas, and those events put you on the path to Australia, where you met your incredible husband Peter and gave birth to two beautiful girls. So in the days to come, in your quiet times, go back there and revisit the experience with awareness. ***Being here, in the reality of this moment is always the biggest healer.***[R]

~ 27 ~

Can you be the space for your experience?

Einstein said *no problem can be solved from the same level of consciousness that created it.* Dr. Rahasya Kraft says *where there is a shift of consciousness, spontaneous healing of anything can and often happens.* Bruce Lipton says *if you change your mind, incurables can be cured instantly.*

I am living proof of what these masters point to. The solution to life's most difficult challenges lies in a new way of seeing, what Einstein, Lipton and Rahasya have referred to as 'a change of mind' and 'a shift of consciousness'. This shift of perspective is always here waiting for you in awareness, which takes you to the other side of resistance to what is here now. Here now is the place we meet our selves and come home again.

[Steven and Lily embrace]

[Beep beep] Lily, my taxi is waiting.

Please take this. *[Steven passes Lily a hand written note]*

What is it?

On my flight down to see you today, I was thinking of you and this poem came through to me. It's something you can sit with from time to time to help you remain aware of the things we talked about today and the bigger perspective of this situation.

Thank you Steven *[Steven and Lily embrace in a long hug]*

Ok, I must run, but I am just a phone call away ... Good luck, Lily.

Goodbye Steven ... thank you.

[As Steven drives off, Lily looks down and reads the note]

I came here today with purpose, not grieving
To bring a new perspective to this life you are living

Challenges come, many sizes and shapes
Their fingerprint the same, despite changing face

Cancer a symbol of things we don't want
Life gets in our face, to dissolve what's distraught

Remember that suffering is not who you are
Pain held by resistance, right here – yet so far

A new way of seeing, for those who are willing
Surrender my friend, let truth be your healing

What's here at this moment is scary, no doubt
Nothing to lose, except a room with lights out

Take a step, look in, fear not the unknown
The unknown plus awareness is your friend not your foe

Experience this moment, and the truth that it brings
For life is for living, your purpose – to sing

There is but one question that remains yours alone
Can you be the space for your experience,
*   and welcome yourself home?*

Life begins where resistance ends

Glossary and
Quick Reference Guide

Atoms – Atoms are the building blocks of everything in the universe. From a simplified scientific perspective, our physical bodies are made up of trillions of cells. These cells are made up of molecules that are groups of atoms bound together. Anything physical is made of atoms. *(See Universe)*

Awakening – A shift of consciousness and perception, where the 'real' you is realised from the higher rungs of consciousness. This state is not something that you get from outside of yourself, it is a revealing of your natural state. When you awaken, your resistances to life fall away and you experience the oneness in all things, from a space of awareness, love, joy and peace that you are. *(See Awareness, Consciousness, Oneness, Resistance, Shift in Consciousness)*

Awareness – A state of presence. A conscious witnessing by which you come to perceive, know, or feel whatever it is that is being witnessed or experienced in that moment. It is impartial, and comes from a stance of openness and acceptance. *(See Experience, Moment, Presence, Resistance, Thinking Mind)*

Cells – *(See Atoms)*

Consciousness – A state of awareness, the state of being aware of one's awareness (self-awareness). Within this state is perception, how we perceive, interact with and experience our reality (life). Anything we are aware of externally or internally at any given moment forms part of our consciousness. The awareness of experience. *(See Awareness, Experience, Perception, Reality, Unconsciousness)*

Consciousness Equation –

Consciousness = Perception = Vibration = State of Health

Decision Point – A critical point in time where people make a conscious decision to live or die.

Disharmony – Discord. Anything in our physical outer life or our inner invisible life that is not in harmony. Disharmony is felt or experienced in such things as: disease, illness, painful or unusual physical symptoms in the body, as well as in our thoughts, feelings, emotions, psyche, and sensations. *(See Harmony, Psyche)*

Dr. Bruce Lipton – www.brucelipton.com/about

Dr. David R. Hawkins M.D. PH.D – www. http://veritaspub.com/about_us.php

Dr. Rahasya Fritjof Kraft – www.livingunity.com/about/

Dr. Ryke Geerd Hamer – www.learninggnm.com/documents/
hamerbio.html

E=mc² – Einstein's equation for Mass-Energy equivalence. The
'Energy Equation'. The equation shows that everything in this
universe is energy, and that all physical things that have a mass
have an energy equivalence. It shows that Matter and Energy are
entwined, two sides to the same coin. *(See Energy & Matter)*

Ego – Our resistance to What Is. It is that part of us which says No
to life and our experiences. It is the false sense of self that seeks to
perpetuate itself by avoiding and fighting with whatever comes
into our reality that threatens the established sense of self. The Ego
also perpetuates itself by projecting an inflated image of itself to
others. *(See Experience, Resistance, What Is)*

Energy & Matter – The visible and invisible forms of what makes
up everything in the universe. Energy & Matter are entwined as
the same-self, two sides to the same coin. Energy is the invisible
form of what makes up everything. Matter is anything that is
physical, occupies space and has a mass. *(See E=mc²)*

Experience – Life happens through our experience in each
moment. Experiences are the elements of life that become our
reality as we meet or avoid What Is. Experience happen in all of
the perceptions of the body and mind such as: thoughts, feelings
and sensations. *(See Life, Reality, What Is)*

Germanic New Medicine (GNM) – The name given to the life's work of German doctor Ryke Geerd Hamer culminating in a book titled *Scientific Chart of Germanic New Medicine.* This work details how unresolved emotional 'Conflict Shock' events, leads to physical conflict mass (disease of the body), such as cancer and other illnesses. www.learninggnm.com/home.html

Grace – A higher power that is always with us and within us. Divine assistance.

Harmony – A physical or mental state of being at peace, in balance, healthy, whole.

Here Now – The present moment. The only thing that exists and is true.

Hurt – A story of the past that holds pain intact by repeating the story.[R] *(See Pain)*

Identity – A sense of self. The thoughts that are formed around who you believe yourself to be. The 'me' you believe yourself to be. The image we have of 'who we are' that we agree with, become attached to, perpetuate and protect. *(See Sense of Self)*

Inner Self – The inner you, your psyche. The world of your invisible thoughts, feelings, beliefs, stories, ideals … *(See Mind, Psyche)*

Intention – Our focused conscious thoughts regarding our goal, purpose or aim. The inner conscious spark that kick-starts what is manifested in life. A potent communication you can initiate with the universe and its greater intelligence. *(See Consciousness, Universe)*

Ladder of Consciousness – The life's work of David R Hawkins M.D. PH.D which is a map detailing the levels and characteristics of Human Consciousness. The full ladder of consciousness can be found in his book title: Power Vs. Force, the hidden determinates of human behaviour. *(See Consciousness, David R. Hawkins M.D. PH.D)*

Life – A succession of experiences that we are here to meet in each moment. *(See Experience)*

Matter & Energy – *(See Energy & Matter)*

Meditation – A state of being with whatever is here right now.

Mind – A bundle of thoughts. A person's mental processes. The inner world of thoughts, stories, identity, beliefs, strategies, ideals, fears, hurts etc. The faculty of reason and thought, by which a person thinks, feels, perceives, reasons, remembers, desires, judges, resists etc. *(See Consciousness, Psyche, Ladder of Consciousness, Thinking Mind)*

Molecules – *(See Atoms)*

Oneness – The unity and interconnectedness of all things.

Outer Self – The outer physical you. The experiences that happen in your outer physical life (relationships, work, financial situation, etc), including the state of health of your physical body and related functions. *(See Life)*

Pain – A part of life that is experienced in our thoughts, feelings, emotions or physical sensations. Physical pain is a sensation you feel in the body. With emotional pain, the physical body might react to the situation with stress, tightness or shock for example, which creates a sensation that the mind calls Pain. Emotional pain is often linked to a story. When we hold onto and repeat a story, Pain becomes ongoing hurt.[R] *(See Hurt)*

Pain Body – A energetic entity that gets lodged in the organs of the body that consists of old emotional pain. It's the accumulation of unresolved emotional hurts that have not been faced or experienced. Resistance is the fuel that perpetuates the Pain Body. *(See Hurt, Pain, Resistance)*

Perception – How we perceive, interact with and experience our reality (life experiences). Perception is interwoven with our realised level of consciousness. *(See Consciousness, Experience, Ladder of Consciousness, Life)*

Presence – A state of being present, being focussed on what is existing or occuring now. A state of witnessing or reflection in the very moment. *(See Here Now, Thinking Mind)*

Present, Past & Future – The current moment, the past moment, and the future moment. The only moment that is true and exists is the present moment. The past no longer exists and the future is only a projection and doesn't exist.

Psyche – The Mind, the deepest thoughts, feelings or beliefs of a person. *(See Mind)*

Realised – Relates to our state of consciousness. The level of consciousness within the human condition that has been realised (is 'real' as per our reality) at any moment of time. *(See Consciousness, Ladder of Consciousness, Reality, Shift of Consciousness)*

Reality – Life as you perceive it based on your realised level of consciousness. *(See Consciousness, Ladder of Consciousness, Life)*

Reflection – A process of looking at oneself. Focused thought or consideration that happens in presence. *(See Presence)*

Resistance – The avoidance of experience. All the ways we avoid or fight with What Is. Resistance is wanting things to be different than it already is. It is a common characteristic found in the lower levels of human consciousness that keeps us stuck and suffering. *(See Experience, Suffering Equation, Unconsciousness, What Is)*

Sense of Self – *(See Identity)*.

Shift of Consciousness – A shift in your realised state of consciousness. A fundamental change in your perception, how you see, interact with and experience reality (life). *(See Awareness, Consciousness, Perception, Realised, Life)*

Society – The structure and often unwritten rules of people living together in an 'orderly' community.

Space – Is everything. Everything in this universe is primarily space made from Atoms which are 99.9% space. Another word for space is Love. *(See Atoms, Universe)*

Spirituality – A process of discovering the true self. A process of de-identification and re-identification of Who I Am. *(See Identity, Realised)*

Story – A bundle of thoughts, memories, ideas and perceptions that are consolidated into an interpretation that we share with others.

Story of Me – The stories we tell ourselves, about ourselves, in relation to others and past experiences that are typically associated with a repeating core theme in our life journey. As we believe and repeat the 'story of me', it solidifies into our sense of self. *(See Identity, Life, Resistance, Sense of Self, Story)*

Stress – The gap between where you are and where you want to be. [R]

Subconscious Mind – A part of the mind that notices and remembers information even when you are not actively trying to do so, and influences your behaviour even though you don't realise it. *(See Awareness, Mind)*

Suffering – A personal state of disharmony. It may appear in the physical as disease for example, or it may be felt as a feeling, sensation in the body or in our mental state. *(See Disharmony, Ego, Resistance, Suffering Equation)*

Suffering equation –

Suffering = experience * resistance

Surrendering – Is a letting go of resistance to What Is. Surrender is not a 'giving up', it is the allowing and experiencing of whatever is here right now without condition. Surrendering is not weakness, it is a great strength of character which promotes healing. *(See Resistance, What Is)*

The Real Self (True Self) – The real you underneath all the inner clouds of unconsciousness that mask the truth. It is the real you at the highest levels of consciousness. *(See Consciousness, Ladder of Consciousness, Unconsciousness)*

The False Self – The separate sense of self that you believe yourself to be. The Ego and all the false identities you adopt, become addicted to and defend. *(See Ego, Identity, Realised, Sense of Self)*

Thinking Mind vs. Working Mind – The Thinking Mind (Ego) is that part of us that resists What Is. The Working Mind is that part of us that is functional, doesn't look at any task as 'good' or 'bad', simply responds in the moment to fulfil the task. *(See Mind, Ego, What Is)*

Trauma – An incredible seducing story for the psyche to hold onto an identity that is not true [R] *(See Identity, Psyche, Story)*

Unconsciousness – The state of not being aware. Characterised by being reactive, automatic and repetitive, and focused on the past or the future but never here now. Unconsciousness is the denial of experience. *(See Awareness, Experience, Here Now, Present Past &* *Future)*

Universe – This existence, all things, the life force, the mysterious source that empowers all things and is entwined in our being. *(See Life)*

Vibration – The gyrating affect of the atoms and molecules that are the building blocks of the universe. The movement back and forth of an object. A person's emotional state. The resonance of the Pain Body. All things are vibration. *(See Atoms, Universe)*

What Is – The way things are, our situation, our inner and outer circumstances, what is here right now, the way life is at this moment, our experience in any given moment of time. *(See Here Now, Present Past & Future)*

A message from the author

Thank you for reading *Inner Sky*. I hope the messages it contains give you new perspective that allows you to break free from whatever binds you.

Please feel free to send a copy of this book to a friend, colleague or acquaintance. If you have obtained a free copy of this book, and have gained something from its wisdom, you are welcome to make a donation at **www.stevenlayer.com**. All donations will be directed towards helping spread the messages found within *Inner Sky*.

With gratitude,

Steven Layer

Acknowledgements

To Roz Hopkins and Natalie Winter (captainhoney.com.au) my deepest gratitude for your exceptional guidance. Thank you for leading me through the publishing process, bringing *Inner Sky* to fruition in such a professional and beautiful way. It is a pleasure and an honour to be associated with such an experienced, focused, and creative organisation.

Laurel Cohn. Thank you for your insightful assessment, structural editing and ongoing guidance. Your in-depth understanding of story structure, flow and editing shaped Inner Sky to be what it is today - a special book that will help many people. I am truly blessed to have found you. Deepest gratitude.

Azriel Re'Shel. Thank you for your superb work in editing *Inner Sky*. I realise that it was a challenging manuscript, filled with many advanced concepts that 'try to explain the unexplainable'. Your knowledge of the subject matter and keen eye are reflected within *Inner Sky*. Thank you kindly.

Steven's grade 5 school photo

About the author

STEVEN LAYER (Premdas) is originally from a small woodsy town outside of Boston Massachusetts in America and now lives in the coastal area of Byron Bay in the far north coast of New South Wales, Australia.

Although holding degrees in Accounting and Information Systems, and owning a number of companies throughout his career as a Systems Engineer, Steven's core interests are life, people and the human condition.

Through numerous challenging life experiences that he investigated with awareness, Steven has realised a certain level of inner and outer freedom. His passion is helping people help themselves, just as he has helped and healed himself.

The second name of Premdas was given to Steven by his teacher and friend Dr. Rahasya Fritjof Kraft. It is an Indian Sanskrit name meaning 'Servant to Love'.

The book *Inner Sky* is a gift, created in this service.

As Dr. Rahasya Fritjof Kraft points out, to be a 'Servant to Love' means you cannot be a 'Servant to the Ego'. You sit at the feet of consciousness, living with awareness of everything that life brings your way.

Inner Sky is Steven's first public written works.
Enjoy!

www.stevenlayer.com

Rahasya and Steven in Dalian, China (2015)
Rahasya's website: **www.livingunity.com**

* 9 7 8 0 6 4 8 0 2 6 6 4 8 *